Gifts from the
Southwest
KITCHEN

by *Judy Walker*
and *Kim MacEachern*

Photographs by
Christopher Marchetti

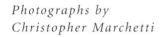

NORTHLAND PUBLISHING

The fifth cookbook with my name upon it is dedicated to Kim MacEachern,
the fabulous cook without whose unending support, friendship, sense of humor,
and inventiveness these books would not exist. — J.W.

My part in this book is entirely the result of the graciousness and friendship
of Judy Walker. Over the years, we have shared some of life's most intimate
moments: weddings, births, and the like; we shared our children and our extended families;
and we shared food. Many of the recipes we have written about are symbols of the life we share.
What an unusual treasure are these records of all the wonderful gifts
Judy has shared with me and my family. — K.M.

© 2001 by Judy Walker and Kim MacEachern
Photographs © 2001 by Christopher Marchetti
All rights reserved.

The text type was set in Minion and Formata
The display type was set in Sphinx Inline
Art Director: David Jenney
Designer: Billie Jo Bishop
Food Stylists: Kathy Cano-Murillo, Michelle Zecchini Cano
Editors: Stephanie Bucholz, Tammy Gales
Production Coordinator: Donna A. Boyd

This book may not be reproduced in whole or in part, by any means (with the exception
of short quotes for the purpose of review), without permission of the publisher.
For information, address Permissions, Northland Publishing,
P. O. Box 1389, Flagstaff, Arizona 86002-1389.

www.northlandpub.com

FIRST IMPRESSION, 2001
ISBN 0-87358-788-X

Composed in the United States of America
Printed in Hong Kong
01 02 03 04 05   5 4 3 2 1

Library of Congress Cataloging-in-Publication Data
Walker, Judy Hille.
Gifts from the Southwest kitchen / by Judy Walker and Kim MacEachern.
p. cm.
1. Cookery, American--Southwestern style. 2. Gifts. I. MacEachern, Kim. II. Title.
TX715.2.S69 W33 2001   641.5979--dc21
2001044157

CONTENTS

ACKNOWLEDGEMENTS

The best recipe for cookbook success is collaboration with friends and family. So many people helped us along the way in this journey, starting with the wonderful staff at Northland Publishing, especially (but not limited to) Dave Jenney, Brad Melton, Lois Rainwater, Kerri Quinn, and Linda Kranz. Thank you, Stephanie Bucholz, for the patient editing job!

Very special props go to the multi-talented Kathy Cano-Murillo, whom Judy had the great fortune to work with at *The Arizona Republic* for several years. Early in her years at that paper, Judy had the opportunity to meet and interview the famous "Make-A-Mix" Ladies: Karine Eliason, Nevada Harward, and the late Madeline Westover. *Make-A-Mix Cookery* and its subsequent editions were one of Judy's inspirations for this book. Another was Anne Byrn, author of *The Cake Mix Doctor*, who gave valuable advice during one of the most fun interviews and food styling experiences Judy ever had.

We also wish to thank Barbara Pool Fenzl, Donna Colletta, Denise Rivers, Sally Stearman (and the rest of the Spa Maidens!), Barbara Yost, Shirley Lohmann (hello, Wilhoit!), Sharon Cooper, Brady Horn, Stacy and Thomas Koch, and Kathy, Russ and Kyle Gerlach, the Roneys, Medlyn/Kammans, and Susan Mathew. All provided recipes, inspiration, valuable assistance or helped consume the fruit of our labors! We adapted part of a salad recipe from our longtime pal, Norman Fierros, of Norman's Arizona, whose cooking has inspired us for years.

In thanking our relatives for their contributions, we must start with our moms, Bobbie Trower and Jacquie Weedon. Both of these beautiful women are constant sources of inspiration and great recipes. We are lucky to be related to them as well as (Aunt) Sarah Staley and Mary (Girl Cuz) Stutsman, who both helped with this book. We can always count on loving support from the Walkers (Bev, Vera, Charlie) and our dads, Walt (Weedon) and Bill (Trower).

The same glowing things could be said about our two kids, the almost-siblings, Melanie MacEachern and Mack Walker, both of whom contribute in countless ways to their mothers' projects. And when we get around to heaping superlatives, there will never be enough for our husbands, Doug MacEachern and Dave Walker.

It's the weekend and you're running out the door to a party. Anybody can make a quick stop at the store to pick up a bottle of wine as a hostess gift—but you, lucky you can bring a jar of Kumquat Marmalade from your own kitchen. That homemade marmalade sends a whole different message: "I thought of you and I took the time to cook for you." Time, the most precious commodity these days, is a most appreciated gift.

We have enjoyed bestowing homemade food gifts for years, either as fully prepared potluck dishes and "sick friend" comfort cuisine, or convenient kits with minimal assembly required. When Kim made the Lentil Rice Soup mix for the staff of professionals she supervised as a Christmas gift, it was a big hit. What better way to soothe the stress of a busy work day than to come home and savor a steaming pot of soup you simply set to simmer from ingredients that were already there?

We've made gifts and treats from the lemons and oranges in our backyards, from the prickly pear fruit that's so abundant in the desert Southwest, from powdered pure New Mexico red chile and Arizona pecans and pistachios. But we know that many of our readers are outside this area. Fortunately, regional ingredients such as these are available in major supermarkets nationwide.

A few minutes are all you need to make many of the gifts in this book. A dozen or so are a little more elaborate, but most only require combining ingredients in unusual, colorful ways. Several of our favorite cooked dishes are made in the microwave, and many recipes make more than one gift, so the time you spend in the kitchen can pay off for several friends. The icons that appear with the recipes give you an idea of the notable aspects of each one, such as how it works or who might like it as a gift.

HOSTESS GIFT	Great-4-Kids	POT LUCK
GIRLFRIEND GIFT	LESS THAN 4 INGREDIENTS	Dont Eat This!
versatile	Comfort food	EVERYBODY LOVES IT
IMPRESSIVE	SHELF STABLE	Festive
GREAT-4-GUYS	Super Easy	elegant
HEAT LOVERS	MICROWAVE	

Recipes also include gift tag information to attach to each of your homemade creations. Rewrite the information onto your own handcrafted or store-bought tag, or photocopy the corresponding tag from the pages beginning on page 81. The tags are designed to look delightful whether copied in color or black-and-white. Finally, just cut along the outer border and attach using tape, string, raffia, ribbon, or even wire.

For those who believe they are lacking in the creativity department, we offer presentation ideas that are a breeze—and fun, too! The recipient will think you're a professional. It's amazing what you can do with a bit of fabric, a handful of raffia, and some magic markers. Even a simple paper bag

and some tissue paper can transform a plain puff-pancake mix into an eye-pleasing package in just minutes. Decorating is also a fun way to spend time with your kids, who will love to help embellish your special gifts.

We have fond recollections of fall evenings spent together in our temporary gift factories, our kitchens, making hearty soup mix and enchilada sauce gifts. While testing recipes for this cookbook, we served many of the results to our own families and also gave many away. In every single case, the recipients were thrilled. We know you will be, too.

Decorating
SUPPLIES
& IDEAS

Getting Started—Tackling a fabulous project doesn't come without a bit of much-needed preparation. The following pages will give you a few tips to make the job easier.

Before you start, clear a workspace large enough to allow for creativity and organized assembly. Line your table with an inexpensive plastic cloth to protect it from stains. Use clear plastic boxes to store and separate supplies. Keep a bottle of window cleaner on hand to remove any stubborn sticky price stickers or labels. A damp sponge and paper towels come in handy to clean up spills before they dry. In addition, a little music in the background does wonders for creative motivation!

Supplies

The best thing about the projects within these pages is that the supplies are common objects that can be used for a variety of purposes.

Scissors—Yes, a standard pair is mandatory, but an additional pair with scalloped blades is just as important. Use them to add a festive trim to a gift card or label. Mini scissors are great for reaching into those hard-to-reach places.

Glue—White glue applied with a brush, a glue stick, or double-sided tape are all appropriate for paper. A tube of E6000 is necessary for porous surfaces and a standard glue gun with all-purpose glue sticks will suffice for everything in between.

Craft knife—You never know when you might need one of these helpful tools.

Paints and varnish—Stick with brush on water-based acrylics and varnish. Not only do they make for easy clean up, but they are also non-toxic and odorless.

Brushes—One package of assorted sizes will be plenty for base coating and outlining. Natural bristles work best on a variety of surfaces. Sponge applicators are fine as a substitute, although they don't offer as much control. When painting, keep a jar of clear water close by for immediate rinsing to prevent brushes from drying with paint on them.

Tape—Double-sided tape will save you in a pinch, but Scotch tape is fine, too.

Pencils and pens—Pencils and/or red china markers will add dimension to signing gift cards or designing decorative labels. Gold and silver paint pens will also add an elegant flair and are great for acenting letters.

Materials

Now that you have all the supplies, it's time to gather the fun items that will pull your designs together. When shopping for decorative materials, think southwestern: bandanas, horses, cacti, coyotes, suns, Native American or Mexican patterns, chili peppers. It's all fair game!

Papers—Invest in a variety of textures, such as colored card stock, handmade papers, vellum, or any other type you would like to incorporate.

Packaging—Head over to the candy-making aisle of your local grocery store to find packages of clear cello bags and twist ties. These will be used for dry ingredients in your projects. For gift baskets, pick up a large bag of excelsior for filler, a roll of clear cello wrap to wrap the basket, and a spool of string for tying off the top of the cello.

Elastic cording is a must-have for attaching fabric to the tops of jar lids.

Raffia—If there is one must-have supply, it has to be raffia, lots of it in as many colors as you can find.

Beads, ribbons, and other knick-knacks—When searching for the perfect final touches, take time to roam the aisles to find materials of different mediums. Most craft stores offer an array of items including ribbon, beads, stickers, fabric, hanging ornaments, conchos, colored leather strips, charms, marbles, rocks, rusted plant pokes, wooden shapes, stencils, rubber stamps, and more. When in doubt, go for dried chile peppers from the grocery store, you can never have too many, and they will fit perfectly with most of your masterpieces!

Containers

Embellishments are nice, but the key to southwestern success is in the presentation. Think out of the gift box (literally) for innovative ways to deliver the goods. Wicker and wooden baskets will do the trick, but line them with festive fabrics or bandanas for an extra edge. When filling a basket, accessorize it with items that will come in handy after the fact. Hand-stamped recipe cards or mini-magnets will prove to the receiver that much thought and care went into your offering.

The delicious vinegars, preserves, and salsas you whip up deserve to be decorated in just as flavorful a manner as your other gifts. Visit home accessory stores to find uniquely shaped bottles and jars. The lids or toppers can be fashioned with stickers, fabric, or paint.

Other ways to dress up completed recipes are to utilize non-traditional gift containers. Your gift recipients will be delighted at the ability to reuse a brass bin, a cowboy hat, a corrugated cardboard bag, a paper mache box, and a stainless steel bucket. The ideas are always fun and endless!

Soups &
SOUP MIXES

Lentil Rice Soup

This adaptation of a recipe from Jane Brody's *Good Food Book* is a favorite of Kim's, because it makes a perfect weekday meal. By using dry ingredients, she made the recipe into a delightful gift.

SOUP MIX:

1 cup brown rice

1 1/2 cups lentils (use 3/4 cup each of
  2 different colors to add eye appeal)

1/2 cup sun-dried tomatoes (dry, not packed in oil)

2 teaspoons granulated chicken bouillon

HERB MIX:

1/4 cup dried chopped onion

1 teaspoon celery seed

1 teaspoon granulated garlic

1/2 teaspoon dried basil

1/2 teaspoon dried oregano

1/2 teaspoon dried thyme

1 bay leaf

ALSO:

2 tablespoons flavored
  red wine vinegar or
  other red or cider
  vinegar

Place brown rice, lentils, sun-dried tomatoes, and bouillon in an airtight container. In a separate airtight container, combine all herb mix ingredients. Place vinegar in a 1-ounce jar and seal tightly. Combine all 3 containers for giving.

Attach the following instructions with the gift or copy the tag on page 81:

TO MAKE LENTIL RICE SOUP:

In a large soup pot, heat 1 tablespoon olive oil and sauté 1 chopped carrot for 3 minutes, stirring constantly. Add herb mix and cook for about 1 minute more. Add 8 cups water and soup mix. Stir to combine. Simmer 45 minutes. Add vinegar, salt, and pepper to taste.   MAKES 8 SERVINGS

DECORATING TIP— *The ingredients for this soup mix fit perfectly in a medium-sized soup bowl. Any bowl will do; however, using glass will allow the colorful layers of the rice and lentils to show through. Package the herb mix in a small plastic bag, using a twist tie for closure. Set aside. Layer the lentils and rice in an alternating fashion. Place the bag of herbs on top and in the center. Spread excelsior along the edge of the saucer, and add a spoon if desired. Wrap in cello and top with raffia. Attach a chili pepper along with a gift tag. Finish it off with colorful campfire stickers applied to the cello.*

Navy Bean Soup

This comforting soup is an ideal gift for a family who can't cook for themselves because of an illness, for kids when Mom or Dad is away on a business trip, or for someone who just needs some love in a pot. It brightens any cold winter day to show up at the door with this steaming, filling meal. Cook it on the stove or transfer it to a slow-cooker after boiling for an all-day simmer.

Heat oil in a stock pot; add onion, garlic, and carrots, and sauté until tender and almost brown. Add broth and beans and bring to a boil. Reduce heat and simmer until beans are tender, about 2 hours (or all day on low if transferred to a slow cooker). Add oregano, basil, and tomatoes and cook 10 more minutes.

MAKES 6 SERVINGS

1 tablespoon olive oil

1 medium onion, chopped

2 cloves garlic, minced

3 carrots, peeled and chopped

8 cups chicken broth (about four
   14 3/4-ounce cans)

1 (16-ounce) bag navy beans, rinsed and sorted

2 teaspoons dried oregano

2 teaspoons dried basil

1 (14 1/2-ounce) can tomatoes

Comfort food

Bean, Pasta, and Sausage Soup

The deep flavor, varied textures, and wonderful colors of this hearty soup make it an outstanding potluck dish. The soup can be made ahead of time, refrigerated in a slow-cooker crock, and then reheated. Add the pasta for about ten minutes of cooking on high, but do this last or it will soak up a lot of broth and overwhelm the soup. To make the soup easier to transport, stretch plastic wrap over the top before you put on the lid.

½ **pound hot or mild Italian sausage, cut into bite-size chunks, skin discarded**
1 **large onion, chopped**
3 **cloves garlic, minced**
1 **large carrot, peeled and chopped**
6 **cups chicken broth (49½-ounce can)**
3 **cups water**
1 **teaspoon dried basil**
1½ **cups white beans, such as Great Northern, sorted and rinsed**

1 **(14½-ounce) can pear-shaped tomatoes, drained and chopped**
1 **cup large pasta shells (or other appropriate shape)**
Freshly grated Parmesan cheese for garnish

POT LUCK

In a large pot over medium-high heat, brown sausage. Add onion, garlic, and carrot. Sauté several minutes, until the onion starts to become translucent. Add broth, water, basil, and beans. Bring to a boil. Simmer until beans are soft, about 2 to 2½ hours, skimming the top occasionally. Add tomatoes and simmer 10 minutes.

Attach the following instructions with the gift or copy the tag on page 89:

TO MAKE BEAN, PASTA, AND SAUSAGE SOUP: Heat soup to boiling. Add pasta and simmer 10 minutes. Serve topped with Parmesan.

MAKES 10 SERVINGS

DECORATING TIP— *Think of how many times you've left a pot or dish at a friend's house after a potluck. No more of that thanks to this affordable soup presentation. Package uncooked pasta in a clear bag. Prepare the rest of the soup ingredients according to the recipe directions. Using a gallon decorative jar, pour the contents inside. Screw lid on tightly. Place a festive bandana over the top of the lid and attach it with elastic cording. Take a piece of string and tie the bag of uncooked pasta to the front. Wrap raffia around the brim and tie into a bow. Use a bright, shiny marble for the center of your bow.*

Potato and Green Chile Soup in a Basket

Give this pantry-friendly basket of ingredients to friends who never have food in their house! Expect a grateful thank-you call the night your gift recipient makes this. The homey flavor is a winner.

COMBINE THE FOLLOWING IN A GIFT BASKET:

1 small onion

1 (4-ounce) can chopped green chiles

2 large potatoes

1 (14½-ounce) can chicken broth (low-sodium is fine)

1 (12-ounce) can evaporated milk (evaporated skim is fine)

Comfort food   GREAT-4-GUYS

Attach the following instructions with the gift or copy the tag on page 81:

TO MAKE POTATO AND GREEN CHILE SOUP:

Dice 2 slices of bacon (or crumble ½ a pound of bulk sausage) into a medium saucepan. Cook until almost browned. Chop the onion and add it along with the undrained green chiles. Cook until onion is translucent. (Drain grease if necessary.) Peel and dice potatoes; add with broth and salt and pepper to taste. Cover and cook over medium heat 10 to 15 minutes, until potato is tender. Lower heat to simmer and add milk. Mash a few potatoes against the side of the pot if you want a thicker soup. Cook until hot; serve.

MAKES 4 SERVINGS

Hearty Barley Soup

You can divide this mix up into twelve cute packets to give as gifts, or keep it on hand to make instant soup in a pinch. Varying the fresh vegetables at cooking time is up to the maker, but the following combo is particularly tasty.

1 (16-ounce) package tiny macaroni (stars
    or alphabets are fun)

1 (16-ounce) bag split peas

1 (16-ounce) bag lentils

1½ cups pearl barley

3 tablespoons dried oregano

4 cups (yes, this is the correct amount)
    dried chopped onion

2 cups long-grain or brown rice

¼ cup dried parsley flakes

Combine all ingredients in a very large bowl. Mix well. To divide for gifts, place 1 cup mix in each of 12 airtight containers.

Attach the following instructions with each gift or copy the tag on page 81:

TO MAKE HEARTY BARLEY SOUP:

Heat 6 cups chicken broth (or 6 cups water and 2 chicken or beef bouillon cubes) to boiling. Add soup mix and simmer 30 minutes. Add 2 chopped carrots, 2 chopped celery stalks, 1½ cups shredded cabbage, and 1 (14½-ounce) can tomatoes with juice. Simmer 20 minutes.

MAKES 6 SERVINGS

Rainbow Soup

What kids don't like about split pea soup is the yucky color! After they see the rainbow of split peas or lentils in this gift jar, they'll beg for the soup. Look for colorful legumes in health-food stores, Indian or Middle Eastern delicatessens, and import stores that sell a lot of food. The peas need to cook longer than the lentils, so, depending on what colors you can find, it's better to use all split peas or all lentils in this mix.

²⁄₃ **cup each of 3 colors of green, red, brown, or**
   yellow lentils or split peas (for a total of 2 cups)
2 teaspoons granulated chicken bouillon
¹⁄₂ **cup dried chopped onion**
1 teaspoon celery seed
1 teaspoon thyme

DECORATING TIP— *This mix works best when presented in a clear jar, so you can see the beautiful array of colors. Layer the peas or lentils in a 12-ounce jar until almost full. You can divide them into ¹⁄₃-cup batches to make 6 layers if you wish. Place the bouillon, dried chopped onion, celery seed, and thyme in a small, zip-top bag. Place the bag gently on top of the layers inside the jar—the bag should not show through once the lid has been sealed. Place the lid firmly over the top of the jar. Finish off the top by placing a colorful piece of fabric over the lid, and secure it with an elastic band. Wrap a few strands of raffia around it, and tie a knot. Attach a silk flower to the knot as a final touch.*

Attach the following instructions with the gift or copy the tag on page 81:

Great-4-Kids **SHELF STABLE**

TO MAKE RAINBOW SOUP:

Chop 3 large or 5 small carrots. In a stockpot over medium heat, sauté the carrots in 1 tablespoon olive oil. Add the contents of the jar and the seasoning mix. Add 7 cups of water and simmer 20 minutes for lentils, 1 hour for split peas.

MAKES 6 SERVINGS

Black Bean Chili in a Basket

This basket contains all the ingredients for a soup that is so hearty, nobody will even notice it doesn't contain meat. (Use vegetarian broth for a veggie pal.) Best of all, it can be done in a slow cooker. Another wonderful addition to this basket is a jar of Red Salsa, page 37.

GREAT-4-GUYS

COMBINE THE FOLLOWING IN A GIFT BASKET:

2 (15-ounce) cans black beans

1 (16-ounce) can crushed tomatoes

1 (14$\frac{1}{2}$-ounce) can chicken or vegetable broth

1 large onion

SEASONING PACKET:

$\frac{1}{2}$ teaspoon garlic powder

2 teaspoons chili powder

1 teaspoon dried oregano

$\frac{1}{2}$ teaspoon ground cumin

$\frac{1}{2}$ teaspoon salt

$\frac{1}{4}$ teaspoon black pepper

Attach the following instructions with the gift or copy the tag on page 81:

TO MAKE BLACK BEAN CHILI:

Chop the onion and combine it with all ingredients in a large, deep pot. Cover and simmer for 30 minutes to 1 hour, adding more liquid if needed; or place ingredients in a slow cooker on low heat for up to 8 hours. Serve with salsa, chopped onion, and shredded cheese if desired.

MAKES 8 TO 10 SERVINGS

White Chili Seasoning Mix

We love to make White Chili and have been known to serve it at parties along with Classic Red Chili and Black Bean Chili. Both the mix and the finished chili make excellent gifts.

2 teaspoons powdered cumin

2 teaspoons white pepper

2 teaspoons oregano

3/4 teaspoon cayenne

1/4 teaspoon ground cloves

Super Easy   **SHELF STABLE**

Combine all ingredients in a small, zip-top bag. To make into a gift basket, combine with 1 large onion, 1 (4-ounce) can chopped green chiles, 3 (14½-ounce) cans chicken broth, and 2 (14½-ounce) cans white beans.

Attach the following instructions with the seasoning packet or basket or copy the tag on page 81:

TO MAKE WHITE CHILI:

In a large, deep pot, heat 1 tablespoon olive oil and sauté 1 chopped onion, 2 cloves minced garlic, contents of seasoning packet, and 4 boneless, skinless chicken breasts, diced. Add a 4-ounce can green chiles, 3 cans chicken broth, and 2 cans drained white beans. Bring to a boil, reduce heat, and simmer 20 minutes. Serve topped with shredded Monterey Jack cheese. Can also be garnished with chopped cilantro, sour cream, and salsa.

MAKES 8 SERVINGS

DECORATING TIP— *You will need a large, heavy-duty basket for this presentation. Tie a Mexican-inspired fabric or bandana around the edges of the basket. Glue in place as needed. Place excelsior into the bottom of the basket. Next wrap the top of each "ingredient can" with raffia and leave a long piece of raffia hanging from each can. Arrange the cans in the basket and then place the onion next to the cans. We think a large, red onion looks best in this presentation basket. Be sure to peel the onion, so that the clean, shiny surface is visible. Place the seasoning ingredients into a clear cello bag. A nice presentation here is to layer the seasoning ingredients into the clear bag. Attach the bag of ingredients to the side of the basket. This basket can be re-used for storing fruits and vegetables.*

Superior Chili Seasoning

This is a great gift for a hunter or a Super Bowl fan! Commercial chili seasoning packets contain things like anti-caking agents. You don't need them; you just need this recipe. The sugar is optional, but recommended because it mellows the tomato acid in the chili. When you make up packets to give away, don't forget to save a couple for yourself!

SINGLE BATCH:

2 tablespoons powdered pure red chile

1 teaspoon garlic powder

$1/2$ teaspoon salt

$1/2$ teaspoon sugar (optional)

$1/4$ teaspoon powdered cumin

$1/4$ teaspoon powdered Mexican oregano

Combine all ingredients in a small, zip-top bag.

MAKES 5 TO 6 SERVINGS

LARGE BATCH:

$2/3$ cup powdered pure red chili

2 tablespoons garlic powder

$2^{1}/2$ teaspoons salt

$2^{1}/2$ teaspoons sugar (optional)

$1^{1}/4$ teaspoons powdered cumin

$1^{1}/4$ teaspoons powdered Mexican oregano

Mix all ingredients well in a small, non-plastic bowl. Spoon 3 tablespoons of the mixture into each of 5 small zip-top bags. Attach directions to each.

MAKES 5 PACKETS

Attach the following instructions with the gift or copy the tag on page 83:

TO MAKE SUPERIOR CHILI:

Heat 2 tablespoons oil in a Dutch oven. Chop 1 large onion and sauté with 2 minced garlic cloves. Add 1 pound ground beef and cook until browned. Drain all fat. Sprinkle in chili seasoning mix and stir well. Add 2 ($14^{1}/2$-ounce) cans tomatoes and 1 cup water or broth. Cook at least 30 minutes.

MAKES 5 TO 6 SERVINGS

Condiments

& SEASONING MIXES

Champagne Mustard

If you can't find champagne vinegar, use white wine vinegar to make this wonderful mustard. It's a great gift at Easter or Thanksgiving, because it goes so well on a sandwich of holiday ham. Look for large quantities of dry mustard powder in bulk at Oriental markets.

⅔ **cup dry mustard powder**

1 **cup sugar**

3 **eggs**

⅔ **cup champagne vinegar**

In a medium bowl, mix dry mustard and sugar with a whisk. Add eggs, beating well after each one. Gradually add vinegar, beating with a mixer or the whisk. Pour into a double boiler over medium-high heat. Whisk continuously until thickened, about 8 to 10 minutes. Pour into small jars. Let cool, cover, and refrigerate.

MAKES ABOUT 1½ CUPS

Southwest Seasoning Mix

These are the classic flavors that bring the Southwest to any dish. Prepare this mix and fill recycled spice jars. Make a clever label and send it to your faraway friends who long for a reminder of the Southwest.

2 **tablespoons cumin**

2 **tablespoons oregano**

2 **tablespoons garlic powder**

Combine ingredients in a small bowl and put in a small jar. This recipe makes about 1½ ounces, enough for one large or two small spice jars.

Attach the following instructions with the gift or copy the tag on page 83:

TO USE SOUTHWEST SEASONING MIX:

Sprinkle mix on generously to enliven chicken dishes, salsas, croutons, soups, and salads.

Enchilada Sauce Mix

If you know anyone who craves Mexican food, this is a perfect gift. The layers look like a sand sculpture in a jar. The ingredients fit perfectly in a clear, 4 x 2½-inch jar with a clamp lid. If you can't find that, use any glass jar with a tight-fitting lid that holds 1 cup of dry ingredients.

6 tablespoons powdered pure red chile
1 tablespoon powdered coriander
1 tablespoon powdered cumin
1 tablespoon powdered oregano
1 tablespoon powdered garlic
1 tablespoon onion powder

 IMPRESSIVE   **EVERYBODY LOVES IT**

Starting and ending with the red chile powder, alternate layers of ingredients in the jar using 1 tablespoon of the red chile powder in between the other ingredients.

Attach the following instructions with the gift or copy the tag on page 83:

TO MAKE ENCHILADA SAUCE:

Combine ¼ cup olive oil and ½ cup flour in a 2-quart saucepan over medium-high heat. Stir to form a paste or roux. Cook until mixture just begins to brown. Add seasoning mix and stir to combine. Slowly whisk in 4 cups water, incorporating each addition to make a smooth, gravylike consistency. Stir in ¼ cup cider vinegar. Bring to a gentle simmer, stirring continuously, and cook for 10 minutes.

MAKES 5 CUPS

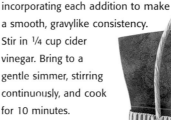

DECORATING TIP— *Not the crafty type? No worries. You can still create a stylish gift with little effort. Layer the dry ingredients into a jar, as stated in the recipe's directions. Top with a faux red chili pepper. Take a bold gift bag, like this corrugated example, and fill it with bright tissue paper and insert the jar. Attach the gift card to the handle.*

Grilled Vegetable Seasoning Mix

This perfect combination of spice and citrus really livens up grilled vegetables. Package the appealing combination of red and orange in a small, clear jar or plastic bag, and present it along with a metal grill basket and long spatula, or add it to a basket of fresh vegetables for grilling, such as eggplant, zucchini, yellow squash, red and yellow bell pepper, carrots, mushrooms, and onions. This recipe makes a little more than ⅓ cup, enough for several pounds of vegetables. It will last several months on the shelf, but will be used up long before that!

Use a tea infuser spoon to uniformly sprinkle on powdered seasoning mixes. (The spoon and seasoning mix make a nice gift combination, too.)

2 tablespoons powdered pure red chile

3 teaspoons powdered coriander

2 tablespoons dried grated orange peel

1 teaspoon salt

 SHELF STABLE

Place all ingredients in a jar or zip-top bag and shake to combine.

Attach the following instructions with the gift or copy the tag on page 83:

TO MAKE SEASONED GRILLED VEGETABLES:

Slice veggies about ⅛-inch thick and lightly spray both sides with oil. Sprinkle with seasoning mix on both sides. Starting with denser vegetables first, adding those with higher moisture content later, grill over medium heat about 10 to 15 minutes, turning once or twice as needed. Mushrooms, except portabellas, take about half as long as other vegetables to grill.

SEASONS SEVERAL
POUNDS OF VEGETABLES

Guava Dressing

This delicate salad dressing is a nice alternative to standard vinegar-based dressings. It is lovely on spring greens with dried cherries, mandarin oranges, sliced red onion, and goat cheese. Try it over diced fruit as well.

1/4 **cup guava nectar**
1/2 **cup mayonnaise**
1 **teaspoon crushed coriander seed**
1/2 **teaspoon dried grated orange peel**

Whirl all ingredients in a blender or whisk together until smooth. Refrigerate.

MAKES 3/4 CUP

Super Easy   IMPRESSIVE

Cilantro Pesto

Whatever you or a lucky gift recipient is making for dinner, this Cilantro Pesto will enhance it. For Southwestern pasta, combine a couple of tablespoons of pesto with hot, buttered linguine. Or stir it into softened butter or mayonnaise and smear it on French bread or sandwiches. It's also great on fish or as a dip. You'll find a dozen other uses.

2 **cups packed cilantro leaves**
2 **tablespoons pine nuts**
1 **tablespoon freshly squeezed lime juice**

elegant

1 **tablespoon minced garlic**
2 **tablespoons freshly grated Parmesan cheese**
Salt and pepper to taste
1/2 **cup olive oil**

In a food processor, combine cilantro, pine nuts, lime juice, garlic, cheese, salt, and pepper. Process until mixture is a paste. While processor is running, slowly drizzle in olive oil until incorporated. Divide into 2 1/2-cup jars to make 2 gifts. Cover and refrigerate. Will keep in refrigerator about 1 week.

MAKES ABOUT 1 CUP

Pickled Garlic

We adore pickled garlic and have been known to make this with the pre-peeled, refrigerated whole garlic cloves you can buy in bulk. To make a spicier version, add three dried chiles to the mix. You can also add sprigs of rosemary, bay leaves, or other herbs. Use this in the Olives Antipasto on page 38, or give it as a gift with instructions for making Pickled Garlic Salad Dressing.

Note: The greatest recent invention for peeling garlic is the rubber tube that takes off the skin. It's easier than smashing the clove with the flat side of a knife, and it leaves the garlic more intact.

HOSTESS GIFT

3 cups peeled fresh garlic cloves

1 ½ cups white distilled vinegar

½ cup sugar

½ teaspoon pickling salt*

3 small dried chiles (optional)

Cut large garlic cloves in half lengthwise. In a 2- or 3-quart non-aluminum saucepan, combine vinegar, sugar, and salt. Bring to a boil and stir until sugar dissolves. Drop garlic into mixture and cook, uncovered, over high heat for 1 minute, stirring occasionally. Remove from heat; let cool. Transfer to ½-pint jars, add dried chiles if using, and cap tightly. Store in the refrigerator. The garlic will be ready to eat in about 5 days, and it will keep well for about 1 year. Makes 3 cups or 3 ½-pint jars.

Attach the following instructions with the gift or copy the tag on page 83:

TO MAKE PICKLED GARLIC SALAD DRESSING:

For the best salad dressing in the world, combine several cloves of this garlic, finely chopped, and a little bit of the liquid from the jar with white wine and balsamic vinegar, extra-virgin olive oil (1 part vinegar to 3 parts oil), and a dab of Dijon mustard. Serve it over a salad of greens, goat cheese, toasted nuts, and chopped pear or apple.

Look for pickling salt with canning supplies. Regular salt has additives that make the brine cloudy.

DECORATING TIP— *A small, round-shaped jar is best to show off this savvy showpiece of pickled garlic. The top can be covered with an ethnic fabric and tied off with ribbon or raffia. Don't forget to attach the gift tag!*

Copper Queen Rub

Any grilled meat will bask in glory as it cooks beneath this zippy rub. For a beefy gift, partner it with barbecue tools and hickory chips.

½ **cup coriander seeds**

1½ **tablespoons dried chopped onion**

1 **tablespoon granulated garlic**

2 **tablespoons dried grated lemon peel**

1 **teaspoon black peppercorns**

1 **teaspoon powdered pure red chile (or chipotle chile powder for extra heat and a smoky flavor)**

1 **teaspoon powdered cumin**

1 **tablespoon salt**

Place all ingredients in a coffee grinder or food processor and reduce to a powder. Transfer to a jar.

Attach the following instructions with the gift or copy the tag on page 83:

TO USE COPPER QUEEN RUB:

Before grilling, rub meat all over with this powder. Let sit for 5 to 10 minutes and then grill as usual.

MAKES ABOUT 1½ CUPS
(SEASONS SEVERAL
POUNDS OF MEAT)

Super Easy   GREAT-4-GUYS

Chile-and-Herb Vinegar

The delicious, deep-red color and front-of-the-mouth heat of this vinegar will add spark to your vinaigrette and spunk to your marinades. The longer you let it steep, the hotter it gets. Use any kind of dried chile or a mixture for layers of flavor.

1 cup dried red chiles, any kind (gently washed if
   needed to remove dust)
4 garlic cloves, peeled and halved
5 sprigs fresh rosemary, or 2 tablespoons dried
3 cups white vinegar

Place chiles, garlic, and rosemary in a quart-size or 1/2-gallon glass jar and crush with a wooden spoon. Heat vinegar in a saucepan over low heat until warm (or in microwave on high power for 1 minute) and pour over chiles and herbs. Close jar, and set on a sunny windowsill for at least 3 days or up to 2 weeks, or until vinegar reaches desired strength. Strain through sieve and pour into 3 sterilized 1/2-pint glass jars. Seal and label. Keeps at room temperature almost indefinitely.

MAKES 3 CUPS

Pomegranate Vinegar

What a beautiful hue this vinegar has! Pair it with the Mango Vinegar (page 27) to complete the Arizona sunset effect.

1 cup pomegranate seeds
1 tablespoon sugar
2 cups rice wine vinegar

Place seeds, sugar, and vinegar in a dry, sterilized jar. Cover and let steep in a cool place for 7 to 10 days. Strain through cheesecloth and discard the solids. Pour into one or two sterilized bottles and seal. Vinegar will keep in a cool, dark place for 2 months or for 6 months refrigerated.

MAKES 2 CUPS

DECORATING TIP— *Vinegar has never been more exciting! Prepare the recipe according to the directions. Pour into a chunky circular bottle. Use a shiny rock to top off the cork. Take two large strips of colored leather and tie into a loose, floppy bow. Tie knots at the bottom of the leather strips. Complete the look with a beaded Native American-style applique. The end result not only tastes great, but makes for a whimsical accent to any kitchen.*

Garnet Glaze

This deeply flavorful glaze for meat and poultry has a silken finish and the color of garnets. It was inspired by the Red Chile Glaze of Texas Chef Jeff Blank. Our version is a little less sweet.

¾ cup chile-and-herb vinegar (recipe page 24)

3 cloves garlic, minced

2 tablespoons minced onion

1 tablespoon dried hot red pepper flakes

1½ cups packed light brown sugar

½ cup soy sauce

1 teaspoon salt

½ cup tomato paste

½ cup (1 stick) butter

IMPRESSIVE

In a skillet, combine vinegar, garlic, onion, red pepper flakes, and brown sugar over medium-high heat and cook until reduced, several minutes. Add soy sauce, salt, and tomato paste and simmer for 5 minutes. Whisk in butter, 1 tablespoon at a time.

Store in refrigerator up to 2 weeks. Use as a glaze for cooked meat and poultry, placing the warmed glaze on each plate under the meat or poultry serving.

MAKES 2½ CUPS

Mango Vinegar

This vinegar is the color of an Arizona sunset. As a gift, it would brighten anyone's day.

3 cups peeled, chopped fresh mango
1 tablespoon sugar
2 cups white wine vinegar

Combine mango, sugar, and vinegar in a dry, sterilized jar. Cover and let steep in a cool place for 4 to 6 days. Strain through cheesecloth and discard the solids. Pour into 1 or 2 sterilized bottles and seal. Vinegar will keep in a cool, dark place for 2 months or for 6 months refrigerated.

MAKES 2 CUPS

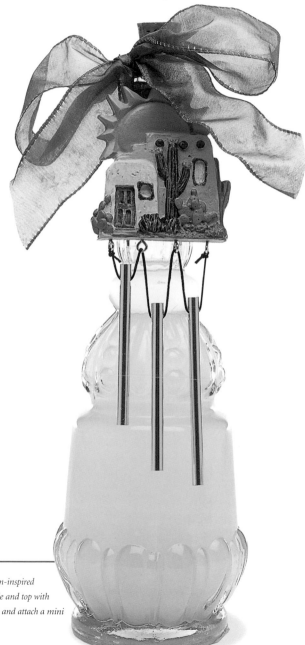

DECORATING TIP— *This sun-drenched liquid looks even more delightful with decorative sun-inspired accents. Prepare the vinegar according to the recipe's directions. Pour into a tall decorative bottle and top with cork. Add a dab of paint to cover the top of the cork. Tie a large bow with thick organza ribbon and attach a mini southwestern wind chime.*

Sloppy Josés Seasoning Mix

Unlike the commercial versions of Sloppy Joes mix, our Southwestern mix is sugar-free. It makes one cup of mix, enough for four gifts of ¼ cup each. Recycled spice jars work well.

¼ **cup dried chopped onion**

4 teaspoons cornstarch

4 tablespoons powdered pure red chile

1 tablespoon ground cumin

1 tablespoon garlic powder

2 teaspoons dried hot red pepper flakes

1½ teaspoons dried Mexican oregano

2 tablespoons salt

Combine all ingredients well in a small bowl. Divide mixture evenly into 4 airtight containers.

Great-4-Kids

Attach the following instructions with the gift or copy the tag on page 85:

TO MAKE SLOPPY JOSÉS:

In a large skillet, brown 1 pound ground beef over medium-high heat with a 4-ounce can of diced green chiles. When meat is browned, drain carefully. To the meat mixture add 1 tablespoon Sloppy José Mix, a 6-ounce can of tomato paste, and 1¼ cups water. Mix well. Cook 10 minutes over low heat. Serve on hamburger buns.

MAKES 4 TO 6 SERVINGS

Cool Sides
& SALSAS

Roasted Peppers Antipasto

This gift is sophisticated and simple at the same time—how can you beat that? We like these gifts for picnics as well as for holiday entertaining. You can make these peppers up to a week ahead; they will keep for about a month refrigerated.

¼ **cup balsamic vinegar**

¼ **cup olive oil**

1 **teaspoon minced garlic**

½ **teaspoon mustard**

⅛ **teaspoon liquid hot sauce**

¼ **teaspoon ground cumin**

1 **teaspoon Italian herb**
   seasoning mix

3 **large red bell peppers, roasted,**
   peeled, and sliced, or 1 (12-ounce)
   jar roasted red peppers,
   drained and sliced

½ **cup slivered red onion**
   (optional)

Super Easy

Combine vinegar, oil, garlic, mustard, hot sauce, cumin, and Italian herbs in a measuring cup or small bowl and whisk well with a fork. Put peppers and onion in a refrigerator container with a lid. Pour the liquid over the peppers and onion, folding gently to distribute evenly. Marinate in the refrigerator at least 8 hours before serving.

MAKES ABOUT 2 CUPS

DECORATING TIP— *Find a uniquely-shaped glass jar with lid for a gourmet presentation. Once filled, the top can be finished with a tie of raffia and a sprig or two of dried chili. This glass jar can cleverly be reused for salsa or flavored vinegars.*

Black Bean and Pasta Salad

The garlic dressing on this salad really makes it sing. What makes it so perfect for a potluck? It tastes best at room temperature. Make the salad three or four hours ahead of time and refrigerate. Remove it from the refrigerator at least half an hour before serving.

1 cup tiny pasta such as orzo, alphabets, or any
  other appropriate theme
2 (19-ounce) cans black beans, drained and rinsed
1 (14¹/₂-ounce) can ready-cut tomatoes, drained
1 small onion, chopped
¹/₂ cup chopped cilantro

DRESSING:
1¹/₂ tablespoons Dijon mustard
3 tablespoons chile-and-herb vinegar
  (recipe page 24)
3 cloves garlic, minced
¹/₂ teaspoon salt
6 tablespoons olive oil

Cook pasta according to package directions and drain well. Combine in a large, portable bowl with drained beans, drained tomatoes, onions, and cilantro.

Prepare the dressing in a separate small bowl by mixing mustard, vinegar, garlic, and salt. Drizzle the olive oil into the mixture and whisk to incorporate. Pour over salad and adjust the salt to taste. Refrigerate. Bring to room temperature before serving.

MAKES 6 LARGE SERVINGS

Comfort food   POT LUCK

Marinated White Beans

This is the salt to the Black Bean and Pasta Salad's pepper. Team the two for the next potluck or Black-and-White theme party, and you will be a hit. This salad also makes a great dip for corn chips.

2 (15-ounce) cans cannellini or Great Northern Beans, drained and rinsed

1 cup chopped red onion

1 large carrot, finely chopped

½ cup chopped parsley

MARINADE:

½ cup olive oil

½ cup rice vinegar

1 teaspoon dried oregano

1 teaspoon dried basil

1 teaspoon dried rosemary

Salt and pepper to taste

In a large bowl, gently stir together beans, onions, carrots, and parsley. In a separate bowl, combine olive oil, vinegar, oregano, basil, and rosemary, crushing the herbs as they are added to the bowl. Add to the bean mixture, stirring to combine. Taste and adjust for salt and pepper. Refrigerate overnight and taste again for salt.* Serve cold.

MAKES 6 TO 8 SERVINGS

* Why should you taste a dish again after it's been refrigerated? Because things that are served cold often need a little more seasoning—the cold can numb the taste buds!

Goat Cheese with Olive Oil and Herbs

This is a wonderful hostess gift or addition to a dinner party. It does take a bit of planning ahead, so if you are giving it as a gift, add a note to indicate when it will be ready to eat.

The oil will solidify somewhat when refrigerated, but will liquefy again upon standing at room temperature. You can enjoy the cheese by itself as an appetizer or serve it in a salad.

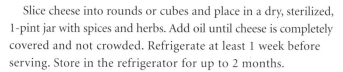

10 ounces firm, fresh feta or goat cheese
4 bay leaves
2 teaspoons rosemary
1 or 2 small, whole dried red chiles
½ teaspoon black peppercorns
Olive oil to cover (about 1½ cups)

elegant

Slice cheese into rounds or cubes and place in a dry, sterilized, 1-pint jar with spices and herbs. Add oil until cheese is completely covered and not crowded. Refrigerate at least 1 week before serving. Store in the refrigerator for up to 2 months.

MAKES 1 PINT

DECORATING TIP—*Make the decor as inviting as the recipe by choosing a strip of ribbon and a paint color to match. Cover the top of the jar lid with the paint, then use a water-based varnish on top to prevent scratches. Spoon the contents into the jar. Screw the lid on tightly. Using a glue gun, attach the ribbon around the edge of the lid.*

Orange Couscous

Coriander is the seed from which cilantro is grown. Kim found it combined with orange peel and termed "Moroccan Coriander." To us, this dish is just as Southwestern as it is Middle Eastern. You can give it to a friend as a mix in a bag or small jar, or make it up and take it to a potluck as is or embellished with finely chopped vegetables of your choice.

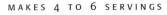

Comfort food

SHELF STABLE

1 cup couscous
2 teaspoons powdered coriander
1 teaspoon dried, grated orange peel
1 tablespoon granulated chicken bouillon or 1 bouillon cube

Combine the couscous, coriander, orange peel, and chicken broth in a medium bowl and stir until mixture is a uniform color. Place in a zip-top bag or ¹/₂-pint jar.

Attach the following instructions with the gift or copy the tag on page 85:

TO MAKE ORANGE COUSCOUS:
Heat 1 cup water to boiling in a small saucepan. Stir in contents of this bag and 2 tablespoons butter. Cook for 2 minutes. Cover, remove from heat, and let stand 5 minutes. Fluff with a fork and enjoy!

M A K E S   4   T O   6   S E R V I N G S

BLACK BEAN SALSA DECORATING TIP— *The festive and creative presentation of this recipe will impress everyone. Start by making the salsa according to the directions. Place into a clear glass jar with a tight lid. Now find a creative container like a cowboy hat or a garden tin—it is nice to give something that can be reused later. Place a bandana or colored cloth inside the container, and secure into place with glue as needed. Place the jar of salsa, along with anything else you would like to add, into the container at varying angles. Stuff raffia, excelsior, or Mexican-colored ribbons around the jars so that they stay in place.*

Black Bean Salsa

This salsa is quick, delicious, and nutritious. It is wonderful as a garnish on Potato and Green Chile Soup or on White Chili (recipes on pages 11 and 15), and it will impress your friends at any party. The best part is that it takes only minutes to make.

1 (15-ounce) can black beans, drained
2 tablespoons chopped red onion
¾ cup chopped tomato
Juice of 1 lime
1 tablespoon chopped green chiles
1 teaspoon sugar
Salt and pepper to taste

Combine all ingredients in a medium bowl. Cover and chill.

MAKES ABOUT 2 ½ CUPS

Super Easy   **POT LUCK**

Salsa Trio

IFor a colorful and festive gift, combine quantities of Tomatillo Salsa, Corn Relish, and Red Salsa in one big basket of southwestern love.

Tomatillo Salsa

Use as a salsa or sauce in many different ways: as a dip or component of guacamole, as a sauce for enchiladas, or pour it over cream cheese.

1 pound tomatillos, husks removed, washed, halved
1 large clove garlic
½ small red onion, cut into chunks
2 serrano or 1 jalapeño chile, quartered, seeds
  removed
1 to 2 tablespoons cilantro leaves
Salt to taste
½ teaspoon sugar
1 teaspoon white vinegar

Put halved tomatillos in a 2-quart microwavable dish with ¼ cup water. Cook on high for 3 minutes. Stir. Cook on high for another 3 minutes. Use hot pads to remove dish from microwave. Drain, saving the liquid.

Put garlic, onion, chiles, and cilantro in the bowl of a food processor and pulse until finely chopped. Add drained tomatillos and pulse until mixture is well blended. To use as a sauce, add saved water to thin the mixture to desired consistency. Add salt, sugar, and vinegar. Taste and adjust seasoning further if needed. Let cool, then cover and refrigerate. Keeps about 1 week.

MAKES ABOUT 2 CUPS

Corn Relish

Corn relish is an old favorite. It can be used as a dip or a side dish. The bright yellow corn dotted with red and green bell pepper gives it special eye appeal, and it tastes as good as it looks.

1 (16-ounce) bag frozen corn, thawed and blanched
   in boiling water, drained
½ cup finely chopped celery
½ cup finely chopped red bell pepper
   (or diced pimentos)
½ cup finely chopped green bell pepper
½ cup finely chopped sweet onion
1 serrano chile, seeded and finely chopped
Juice of 2 limes
2 tablespoons white vinegar
1 tablespoon sugar
Salt and pepper to taste

In a large bowl, combine corn, celery, peppers, onion, and chile. In a separate small bowl, combine lime juice, vinegar, and sugar. Mix well and pour over corn mixture. Add salt and pepper to taste. Mix well. Refrigerate. Serve cold or at room temperature.

MAKES ABOUT 4 CUPS

Red Salsa

This is the real deal. Oregano is an herb widely used in Mexico, where there are many different varieties. But if you don't care for the flavor, leave it out.

3 ripe tomatoes, diced, or 1 (15-ounce) can diced
   tomatoes
1 onion, finely chopped
2 tablespoons finely chopped cilantro
1 (4-ounce) can chopped green chiles
2 cloves garlic, minced (½ teaspoon)
2 teaspoons red wine vinegar
1 tablespoon olive oil
½ teaspoon Mexican oregano, crushed or
   powdered (optional)

Combine all ingredients in a medium bowl. Refrigerate and chill well before serving.

MAKES ABOUT 3 CUPS

FESTIVE

Olives Antipasto

Is this ever gilding the lily! Use the Pickled Garlic on page 22, and any kind of olives. The more variety the better, but it's good even with just three types. We most often make it with Kalamata olives, cracked green olives, and Greek black olives. To make it a little more "picante," add about ½ teaspoon red pepper flakes.

4 to 6 cups mixed olives

1 small (3 ½-ounce) jar capers, about ⅓ cup

⅔ cup pickled garlic (spicy or sweet is fine)

½ to 1 cup sun-dried tomatoes packed in oil, drained and cut into quarters

1 tablespoon mixed Italian herb seasoning

1 tablespoon chopped parsley

1 teaspoon rosemary

Olive oil to cover olives about halfway

Combine all ingredients except olive oil in an 8-cup container that has a tight lid. Fold together gently but thoroughly. Pour enough olive oil over the mixture to fill the bowl halfway. Cover and refrigerate. Stir or shake gently every now and then as it marinates. Olive oil may congeal during refrigeration; let sit at room temperature for a couple of hours before serving. Will keep at least 2 weeks refrigerated.

MAKES ABOUT 6 TO 8 CUPS

IMPRESSIVE

DECORATING TIP—*For this recipe, go with the old adage that says, "sometimes less is more." This antipasto looks so good by itself that it should be presented in a simply designed clear jar. Wrap a thin strip of corrugated cardboard around the jar and glue into place. Place two nice pieces of wheat or barley into the cardboard wrap and secure with another dab of glue. Seal tightly, and wrap the top with a few strips of raffia or colored cloth. Now it's ready to give to that special somebody!*

Breads &
BREAD MIXES

Real Cornbread Mix

We call this Real Cornbread because it's the real thing—not too sweet, not too dry, just right. A bag of this mixture is a great addition to the Black Bean Chili Basket (page 14) or any of the soups and soup mixes beginning on page 7. You can use any type of cornmeal in this: white, yellow, or blue. We like stone-ground meal of all colors.

¾ **cup all-purpose flour**
1½ **cups cornmeal**
1 **teaspoon salt**
4 **teaspoons baking powder**
3 **tablespoons sugar**

Stir together in a medium bowl the flour, cornmeal, salt, baking powder, and sugar. Package in a zip-top sandwich bag.

Comfort food

Attach the following instructions with the gift or copy the tag on page 85:

TO MAKE REAL CORNBREAD:

Preheat oven to 400 degrees.

Combine 1¼ cups milk and ¼ cup vegetable oil in a large bowl. Add 2 eggs and beat well. Dump cornbread mix into a separate large bowl. Stir egg mixture into cornbread mix until smooth. Pour into a greased 9 x 13 pan, a 10-inch cast-iron skillet, or 10 to 12 individual cast-iron molds. Bake 30 minutes for pans, 20 minutes for molds, until medium golden brown.

MAKES 10 TO 12 SERVINGS

Nut Bread

You will love giving these easy, delicious breads as gifts and making them for yourself. There are many variations, and you can come up with your own special combinations of fruit and nuts. Here we give two of our favorites, as well as some general guidelines for you to go off on your own. Use a sharp, thin knife to prevent crumbling when you cut nut breads.

3 cups buttermilk baking mix (such as Bisquick)
½ cup sugar
1 egg
1¼ cups milk
1½ cups chopped nuts (any kind)

EVERYBODY LOVES IT

Festive

Preheat oven to 350 degrees.

In a large bowl, combine baking mix, sugar, egg, and milk. Beat well for 30 seconds. Stir in the nuts. Pour into a well-greased 9 x 5 x 3-inch loaf pan and bake 45 to 55 minutes, or pour into 6 well-greased 4¾ x 2⅝ x 1½-inch loaf pans and bake about 35 minutes, until toothpick inserted in the center comes out clean. Cool before slicing.

EACH FULL LOAF MAKES 12 TO 16 SERVINGS;
MINI LOAVES MAKE 2 TO 3 SERVINGS EACH

Variations

➤ Use 1 cup banana, unsweetened applesauce, or canned pumpkin, plus ½ cup milk; increase sugar to ⅔ cup and decrease nuts to ¾ cup.

➤ Add 1 cup candied or dried cherries or other dried fruit or berries and decrease nuts to ¾ cup.

➤ Add 1½ cups orange juice and 2 tablespoons grated rind and decrease nuts to ¾ cup.

DECORATING TIP— *Fun and easy gift containers can be made from small paper gift boxes available at most craft stores. Using your glue gun, attach festive chiles and ribbons to the outside of the box. Fill the inside of the box with raffia, and this will cradle your nut bread until it reaches it's destination! Close up the box with a nice big bow.*

Chili Beer-Bread Mix

This version of the forever-popular Beer Bread uses chili powder, unlike other recipes in this book, which call for powdered pure red chile. The difference is that the chili powder you buy in the supermarket has other spices and herbs added to it. The powdered pure red chile is the ground form of red chiles with nothing else added.

Guys love this recipe so much you may want to make a six-pack of Chili Beer Bread mix to give away. Just multiply the ingredients by six and mix in a very large bowl. Divide into 3⅝ cup portions for each bag.

3 cups self-rising flour*
3 tablespoons sugar
2 teaspoons chili powder
1 teaspoon cumin seed

GREAT-4-GUYS

* Self-rising flour has baking powder already added to the mix. Look for it in the supermarket flour aisle.

Mix together flour, sugar, chili powder, and cumin seed, and place in a small gift bag.

Attach the following instructions with the gift or copy the tag on page 85:

TO MAKE CHILI BEER BREAD:

Preheat oven to 400 degrees. Pour bread mix into a bowl and make a well in the center. Pour in 12 ounces of beer at room temperature. Stir lightly, just until blended. Scrape into a well-greased loaf pan and bake 20 minutes. Remove from oven and pour ¼ cup melted butter over the top. Bake 20 minutes longer.

MAKES 1 LOAF

DECORATING TIP— *For that guy who has everything, how about giving a six-pack of chili beer bread? Using an empty six pack container, glue "chili inspired" fabric to the sides and bottom. Fill the six sections with excelsior. Divide bread ingredients into six parts and place into six clear cello bags. Tie each bag with jute or leather strips (found at most craft stores). Small plastic beer bottles attached at the top of each bag are a nice touch! Bottoms up!*

Bagel Toasts

To make a homemade dipper to give with your favorite spreads such as hummus, dips, or salsas, choose any kind of plain or savory bagel. These are a quick addition to a gift basket or bag.

Super Easy

2 bagels, any savory flavor or variety, such as sourdough, pesto, sundried tomato, etc.

Preheat oven to 300 degrees.

Slice the bagels vertically to make about 18 thin disks per bagel. Place on a baking sheet and bake until dry and hard, about 10 minutes. Cool on racks.

MAKES ABOUT 36 TOASTS

Pumpkin Pistachio Bread

3 cups buttermilk baking mix (such as Bisquick)

2/3 cup sugar

1 egg

1/2 cup milk

1 cup pumpkin

3/4 cup coarsely chopped pistachios

EVERYBODY LOVES IT Festive

Preheat oven to 350 degrees.

In a large bowl, combine baking mix, sugar, egg, milk, and pumpkin. Beat well for 30 seconds. Stir in the pistachios. Pour into a well-greased 9 x 5 x 3-inch loaf pan. Bake 45 to 55 minutes, until toothpick inserted in the center comes out clean. Cool before slicing.

MAKES 12 TO 16 SERVINGS

Orange Pecam Bread

3 cups buttermilk baking mix (such as Bisquick)

²/₃ cup sugar

1 egg

1¼ cups orange juice

2 tablespoons grated orange rind

¾ cup coarsely chopped pecans

Festive

Preheat oven to 350 degrees.

In a large bowl, combine baking mix, sugar, egg, orange juice, and rind. Beat well for 30 seconds. Stir in the pecans. Pour into a well-greased 9 x 5 x 3-inch loaf pan. Bake 45 to 55 minutes, until toothpick inserted in the center comes out clean. Cool before slicing.

MAKES 12 TO 16 SERVINGS

BUTTERMILK CURRANT SCONE MIX DECORATING TIP— *A one-of-a-kind bread basket that will be treasured for years to come is easier to make than you might think. Purchase a rectangular-shaped flat basket with side handles. Wrap colorful western-inspired ribbons around the bottom edge of the basket. At your local craft store purchase twenty or so polished rocks in colors that will coordinate with your ribbon selection and also a package of plastic copper-colored beads. Glue the rocks around the top edge of the basket, and the copper beads can be applied to the tops of the handles. Fill the basket with excelsior and then place your scones or bread on top. This is truly a one of a kind bread basket!*

Buttermilk Currant Scone Mix

As a breakfast classic or during afternoon tea, these scones are so fun to roll out and cut up. Children love them anytime. If you don't have dried currants handy, substitute golden raisins.

2½ cups buttermilk baking mix
2 tablespoons sugar
½ cup dried currants

Great-4-Kids

In a medium bowl, stir together buttermilk baking mix and sugar. Package in an airtight container such as a zip-top plastic bag. Put currants in a snack-size plastic bag. Package the 2 elements together in a gift bag.

Attach the following instructions with the gift or copy the tag on page 89:

TO MAKE BUTTERMILK CURRANT SCONES:
Preheat oven to 450 degrees. Put dry mixture into a large bowl. Use a knife to cut 6 tablespoons of very cold butter into small pieces, adding it to the mix. Use a pastry cutter or 2 knives to cut the butter into the mixture until it resembles coarse crumbs. Beat together 2 eggs with milk and add to the mixture along with currants. Mix until the liquid is completely incorporated. Dough will be very soft.

Turn out onto a heavily floured surface and knead gently, turning the dough 5 or 6 times. Pat out with your hands into a 9-inch square. Cut into 3 rectangles. Cut each rectangle in half, then cut each half into triangles. Place on a lightly greased jelly roll pan 1 inch apart. Brush tops with 1 tablespoon of milk and sprinkle with 1 tablespoon of sugar. Bake 12 to 15 minutes, until tops are lightly golden.

MAKES 12 SCONES

Puff Pancake Mix

We love Puff Pancakes, also known as Dutch Baby or German pancakes, because they're dramatic, light, and different. They're great topped with cut-up fruit—especially sliced strawberries or fruit syrup. They can also be sprinkled with lemon juice and powdered sugar. This recipe makes seven mixes to give away.

1 cup dry buttermilk powder*
4 cups all-purpose flour
¼ cup sugar

4 teaspoons baking powder
2 teaspoons baking soda
1 teaspoon salt

* Look for dry buttermilk powder in the baking aisle at the supermarket. Saco is one common brand.

Combine all ingredients in a large bowl and stir until well mixed. Put ⅔ cup each into 7 snack-size zip-top bags.

Attach the following instructions with the gift or copy the tag on page 85:

TO MAKE PUFF PANCAKES:

Preheat oven to 450 degrees. Put 2 tablespoons butter in each of 2 (9-inch) pie plates, and place in oven to melt. Combine pancake mix, 4 eggs, and ⅔ cup milk in a blender and mix. Batter will be thin. Pour into pie plates and bake 18 minutes, or until pancakes puff up and brown. Remove from oven and sprinkle with lemon juice and powdered sugar, or top with fresh fruit mixed with a little sour cream. Cut into wedges and serve immediately.

MAKES 2 LARGE PANCAKES OR 4 SERVINGS

Great-4-Kids

DECORATING TIP—*A unique way to deliver your puff pancake mix is to decorate a miniature wooden crate. Colorful ribbons or fabric can be wrapped around the outer edge of the crate and finished with a ribbon bow or raffia bow on the front edge. Place silk desert flowers or foliage at the back section of the crate. When the pancake mix has been all served up, this unusual wooden crate looks great filled with a dried flower arrangement!*

Old-Fashioned Oat Cakes Mix

Do you ever wonder, "What did the pioneers give as gifts?" Our guess is that they gave one another baking mixes, like this one for oat cakes, a favorite comfort food of ours. We imagine that, in the Southwest, Prickly Pear Jelly (page 62) often came along with the oat cake mix.

Use a wire whisk to combine mix ingredients. This technique ensures even distribution of the various ingredients throughout the mix.

2 cups all-purpose flour
1 1/2 cups old-fashioned oats
1/2 cup packed brown sugar
1 teaspoon salt
1/2 teaspoon baking soda

In a medium bowl, combine flour, oats, brown sugar, salt, and baking soda. Mix well and place in a zip-top bag.

Attach the following instructions with the gift or copy the tag on page 87:

TO MAKE OLD-FASHIONED OAT CAKES:
Preheat oven to 375 degrees.

Empty bag of mix into a medium-sized bowl. With a pastry cutter or 2 knives, cut in 3/4 cup butter (1 1/2 sticks) until the mixture has a crumbly texture. Add 1/2 cup water or milk and stir with a fork until dough just clings together. Divide dough into thirds and roll out each portion on a lightly floured board to 1/8-inch thick. Cut into 2-inch squares and place 1 inch apart on an ungreased cookie sheet. Bake 10 to 15 minutes, until lightly browned.

MAKES 4 TO 5 DOZEN OAT CAKES

Banana Sour Cream Bread

This bread is light years beyond any banana bread you've ever known. The delicate texture of this variation on an old favorite is so wonderful that the lucky recipient may think you have given them a cake.

1 cup pecans

¼ cup brown sugar

½ teaspoon cinnamon

½ cup vegetable shortening

1 cup sugar

2 eggs

3 ripe bananas, mashed, about 1½ cups

½ teaspoon vanilla

½ cup sour cream

2 cups all-purpose flour

1 teaspoon baking powder

1 teaspoon baking soda

½ cup raisins (preferably golden)

EVERYBODY LOVES IT

IMPRESSIVE

Preheat oven to 350 degrees. Grease or coat well a 6½-cup ring mold or tube pan with cooking spray.

In the bowl of a food processor, combine pecans, brown sugar, and cinnamon. Pulse until just chopped. Spoon ½ the nut mixture evenly around the bottom of the pan and save the rest.

In a mixing bowl, beat shortening and sugar until mixture looks fluffy. At medium speed, beat in eggs, bananas, and vanilla. Add sour cream and blend on low speed for 1 minute.

In another medium bowl, stir together flour, baking powder, and baking soda. With mixer on low speed, gradually add to banana mixture. Beat until well incorporated, stopping once to scrape down batter on the sides of the bowl. Pour ½ the batter over the nut mixture in the pan. Sprinkle evenly with remaining nut mixture, then raisins. Cover with remaining batter and smooth the top gently with a spatula.

Bake for 50 to 55 minutes, until a toothpick inserted near the center comes out with few or no crumbs. Cool for 5 minutes on a rack, then invert pan onto a plate.

MAKES 12 TO 16 SERVINGS

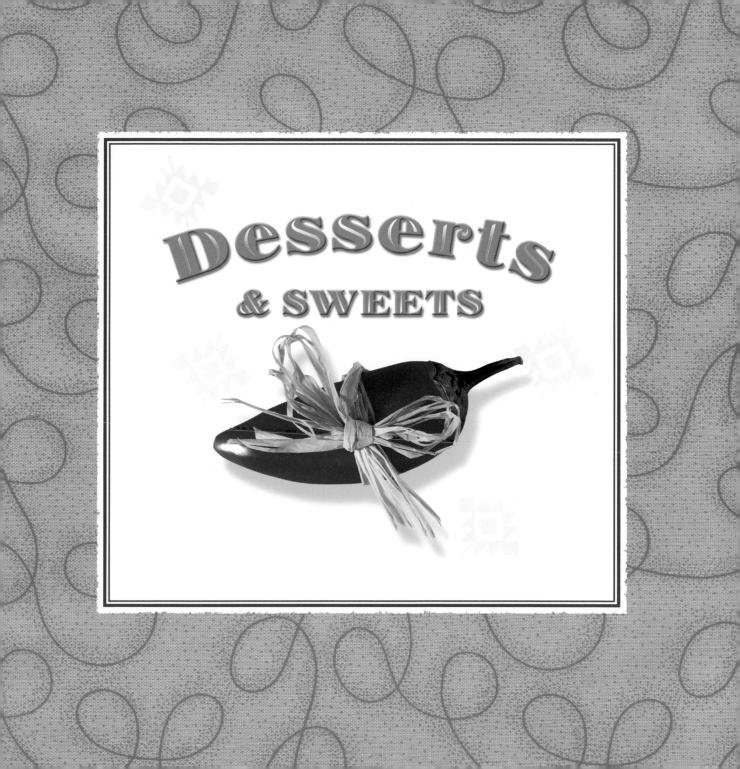

Desserts

& SWEETS

Sand Art Bars

This is the recipe that inspired this cookbook! Sand Art Bars are such a fun thing to make and to give as gifts. People are knocked out by the look of this gift, and the brownie-like result is a sure crowd-pleaser.

1 cup plus 2 tablespoons all-purpose flour
²/₃ **teaspoon salt**
½ **teaspoon baking soda**
²/₃ **cup brown sugar**
²/₃ **cup granulated sugar**
⅓ **cup cocoa**
½ **cup coconut**
½ **cup chocolate chips**
½ **cup chopped nuts**

Great-4-Kids

Layer ingredients in a 1-quart jar in the order given, starting with flour. Shake the jars very gently to level the contents as you add the layers. Crumble the packed brown sugar lightly in your fingers as you add it, then tamp down a bit with the bottom of a ladle. As you get to the top of the jar, press the ingredients down with your fingers if needed.

Attach the following instructions with the gift or copy the tag on page 87:

TO MAKE SAND ART BARS:

Preheat oven to 350 degrees.

Dump contents of jar into a large bowl. Add 3 eggs, ½ cup oil, and 1 teaspoon vanilla. Mix well. Spread into a greased 9 x 13-inch pan. Bake for 27 to 32 minutes.

MAKES 15 TO 18 BARS

DECORATING TIP—*Here are a few hints for packaging the following sweet gifts. These recipes work well in wide-mouth quart jars, normal-size quart jars, mayonnaise jars, or spaghetti sauce jars. We have used all of the above. Pack the top layers down lightly with your fingers if you need to do so, or add a few more nuts, chips, or whatever is in the top layer. A canning funnel is useful if you're filling several jars at a time. If you don't have one, fold a 16-inch sheet of waxed paper in half and twist to form a cone. Staple near the wide end and trim the narrow end to the size of the mouth of the jar. Place each ingredient in the "funnel" as you fill the jar. Cocoa, flour, and buttermilk baking mix (Bisquick) tend to stick to the sides of the jar a little more than the heavier ingredients. You can use a small spatula to neaten up the edges, or wad up a bit of paper towel on the end of a chopstick to use as a swab and to move ingredients around.*

Oatmeal Bars in a Jar

The "bars in jars" rage is going strong in our gift department. This recipe includes mini M&M's baking bits, so kids will just love them.

½ **cup old-fashioned oats**
¾ **cup mini M&M's baking bits**
2 **cups buttermilk baking mix (such as Bisquick)**
½ **cup packed light brown sugar**
½ **cup packed dark brown sugar**

Layer the ingredients in a 1-quart jar as follows: oats, ½ cup M&M's, 1 cup baking mix, light brown sugar, 1 cup baking mix, dark brown sugar, remaining M&M's. Crumble the packed brown sugar lightly in your fingers as you add it, then tamp down a bit with the bottom of a ladle. As you get to the top of the jar, press the ingredients down with your fingers if needed.

Attach the following instructions with the gift or copy the tag on page 87:

TO MAKE OATMEAL BARS IN A JAR
Preheat oven to 350 degrees.
Pour contents of jar into a medium-size mixing bowl. Add ⅓ cup oil, 1 large egg, and 1 teaspoon vanilla. Stir to combine. Press into a greased 8 x 8-inch baking pan. Bake for 20 to 30 minutes or until brown and set in the middle.

MAKES 16 SMALL OR 9 LARGE BARS

EVERYBODY LOVES IT   Great-4-Kids

DECORATING TIP— *A mayonnaise or cookie jar will work wonders for this crafty project. Paint the top of the jar lid with a bright acrylic, then apply a water-based varnish to prevent scratches. Attach a wood sun ornament. Layer the dry ingredients into the jar according to the recipe's directions. Attach lid and seal tightly. Tie various colors of raffia or leather around the brim and attach the gift card with directions.*

Pecan Butterscotch Bars

This installment in the "bars in jars" repertoire features the yummy combination of butterscotch with pecans, a long-time staple of Southwestern farming. Kim's uncle would spend every Thanksgiving on the Yuma farm picking pecans.

To toast the pecans for deeper flavor, microwave them on high for 4 to 5 minutes, stirring every minute; or place on a toaster-oven rack at 400 degrees and cook for several minutes, stirring every minute. To avoid burns, be sure to pull the rack out of the oven when stirring.

¾ cup butterscotch chips
2 cups buttermilk baking mix (such as Bisquick)
½ cup packed light brown sugar
½ cup packed dark brown sugar
½ cup pecans

Super Easy

Layer the ingredients in a 1-quart jar as follows: ½ cup of chips, 1 cup baking mix, light brown sugar, 1 cup baking mix, dark brown sugar, pecans, and remaining chips. Crumble the packed brown sugar lightly in your fingers as you add it, then tamp down a bit with the bottom of a ladle. As you get to the top of the jar, press the ingredients down with your fingers if needed.

Attach the following instructions with the gift or copy the tag on page 87:

TO MAKE PECAN BUTTERSCOTCH BARS:
Preheat oven to 350 degrees.

Pour contents of jar into a medium-size mixing bowl. Add ⅓ cup oil, 1 large egg, and 1 teaspoon vanilla. Stir to combine. Press into a greased 8 x 8-inch baking dish. Bake for 20 to 30 minutes or until brown and set in the middle.

MAKES 16 SMALL OR 9 LARGE BARS

Cake Mix Cookies

Want to mix up a batch of cookies for a favorite friend—or favorite kid—in three minutes flat? Judy has had this recipe since 1986 and loves it for its versatility. It has less fat than some recipes of this kind, and the creative possibilities are endless. Use devil's food cake mix and good-quality chocolate chips to make Double Chocolate Chip Cookies, or try a spice cake mix with chopped walnuts and raisins.

2 eggs
⅓ cup oil
1 teaspoon vanilla   *Super Easy*   Great-4-Kids
  or other flavor
  extract to match or complement the cake mix
1 (1 pound, 2¼-ounce) package cake mix, any flavor

Preheat oven to 375 degrees.

In a large mixing bowl, beat together eggs, oil, extract, and cake mix. Beat 1 minute, then use a spatula to scrape down the sides and bottom of the bowl. Beat 1 more minute, until batter is smooth. Batter will be thick. Stir in the chocolate chips, nuts, or raisins by hand.

Drop cookie dough by rounded teaspoons about 2 inches apart onto ungreased baking sheets. Bake for 10 to 12 minutes or until bottoms just begin to brown. Centers will be soft. Let cookies cool 1 minute on pans before transferring to racks to cool completely.

Variation

Add one 6-ounce package (about 1 cup) semisweet chocolate chips, or ½ to ¾ cup chopped nuts, shredded coconut, or raisins.

MAKES 4 DOZEN COOKIES

World's Best Fudge

The trick to super-simple recipes is to use the best ingredients. It really makes a difference. For this recipe, use the best chocolate chips you can find. We prefer the Ghirardelli brand. You can also get creative; mix semi-sweet, milk chocolate, and butterscotch chips for a less intense, multilayered flavor. And be sure you use the freshest pecans for the decorative topping.

The "very large bowl" mentioned in the recipe is necessary because the marshmallow creme likes to expand as it cooks!

Judy gives away multiple pounds of this fudge every year.

30 ounces best-quality semisweet chocolate chips, or a combination of 12 ounces semisweet chocolate chips, 12 ounces milk chocolate chips, and 6 ounces butterscotch chips

1 (7-ounce) jar marshmallow creme

1 (14-ounce) can sweetened condensed milk (not evaporated milk)

1 cup whole pecan halves*

MICROWAVE

Begin by spraying an 8 x 8-inch baking pan with non-stick cooking spray.

In a very large microwavable bowl, stir together the chips, marshmallow creme, and sweetened condensed milk. Microwave on high 2 minutes, then stir. Microwave another 2 minutes on high and stir again, very well, until mixture is smooth and well-blended. If not completely mixed and melted, microwave on high again for an additional 1 or 2 minutes. Stir again and turn mixture into prepared pan. Mixture will be very thick. Smooth surface with spatula.

Place pecan halves in neat rows across the top, closely spaced but not touching, pressing down lightly into the fudge. Refrigerate until firm, then cut into squares with one nut half atop each piece. Cover and refrigerate for storage, as nuts will stay fresh at room temperature for only 3 or 4 days.

MAKES ABOUT 2 ½ POUNDS

Nuts may be chopped and incorporated into the entire batch. Stir them in during the last microwave cycle.

Apricot Nuggets

Judy's mom, Bobbie Trower, has made this recipe for the holidays for decades. Judy was delighted to find several key ingredients right in her Arizona backyard. This is a great no-bake treat, and like all dishes made with dried fruits and spices, the flavor improves with mellowing.

1 (16-ounce) box powdered sugar

6 tablespoons butter, melted

2 tablespoons orange juice

½ teaspoon vanilla

1 (11-ounce) package dried apricots, ground in a
   food processor to make 1½ cups

1 cup chopped pecans

Combine sugar, butter, orange juice, and vanilla in a large bowl. Add apricots. Mix, then knead with your hands until well mixed. Form into 1-inch balls and roll in nuts.

Store in refrigerator in a covered container.

Variation

Substitute 1½ cups shredded coconut for pecans.

MAKES ABOUT 6 DOZEN

Chile Pecan Brittle

Oh-my-goodness, is this ever good! We have to stop ourselves from making this brittle every day that we have nuts in the house. We have to stop ourselves from breaking off just one more little bite to nibble on. We have to stop ourselves—you get the idea.

Inspiration for this brittle is from Carol Medina Maze's excellent *Mexican Microwave Cookery*.

One warning, though—do not attempt to make this recipe in a plastic container. Judy has somehow managed to melt Tupperware while making candy in the microwave. And for easier cleanup, run hot water into the mixing bowl as soon as you've transferred the brittle to the pan.

1 cup pecan halves

1 teaspoon canola oil

2 teaspoons powdered pure red chile

¼ teaspoon salt

1 cup sugar

½ cup light corn syrup

1 teaspoon butter

1 teaspoon baking soda

MICROWAVE

Combine nuts, oil, chile powder, and salt on a glass pie plate. Microwave on high for 1 minute. Stir, then microwave on high another minute. Set aside.

Coat a baking sheet well with nonstick spray.

Combine sugar and corn syrup in a very large glass microwaveable bowl. Microwave on high 6 minutes, stirring after 3 minutes. Stir in butter and microwave on high 1 minute. Immediately stir in baking soda. Add nut mixture; stir until light and foamy. Pour mixture onto prepared baking sheet. Mixture will be hot. Carefully use your buttered hands, a buttered rolling pin, or a large spoon to flatten the candy and separate the nuts. Let stand until cool, then break into pieces.

MAKES ABOUT 1 POUND

Chocolate Pecan Clusters

This recipe is a family favorite. Kim's Grandma Winnie made peanut clusters every Christmas and now her mother, Jacquie, and Aunt Sarah carry on the tradition. Melanie, Kim's daughter, puts her own spin on this chocolate favorite by changing the nuts to toasted pecans, a more indigenous flavor. See toasting directions on page 78.

Line a baking sheet or 2-foot section of kitchen counter with waxed paper.

Melt chocolate according to package directions. Stir in pecans. Spoon out onto sheets of waxed paper in clumps containing 2 or 3 pecan halves. Let cool about 30 minutes.

MAKES ABOUT 45 CLUSTERS

16 ounces candy-making or dipping chocolate
2 cups pecan halves, toasted

Festive

DECORATING TIP— *Yummy chocolates deserve a delightful candy dish! In this case, a lavish candleholder did the trick. Embellish the outer rim with paints, and colored marbles in an appealing design. Wrap the candies in cello, and tie a rafia bow at the top. Fill the dish with shredded raffia and place the bag of sweets in the center.*

Lemon Pecan Pound Cake

Some people love chocolate, some love lemons. This cake sways the chocolate-lovers over to the lemon side.

The stiff batter in this recipe demands a heavy-duty, stationary mixer.

4 cups all-purpose flour

1 teaspoon baking powder

1 pound (4 sticks) butter, softened

2 cups sugar

6 eggs, separated, at room temperature

Grated rind of 1 large lemon

½ cup freshly squeezed lemon juice

2½ cups white raisins

3 cups chopped pecans, toasted

⅛ teaspoon cream of tartar

Powdered sugar for the top (optional)

EVERYBODY LOVES IT **Festive**

Preheat oven to 275 degrees.

Coat a 10-inch tube or bundt pan with nonstick spray. Stir together flour and baking powder in a medium bowl.

In the large mixing bowl of a stationary mixer, beat butter. Gradually add sugar and continue beating until mixture is light and fluffy.

Add egg yolks, one at a time, beating well after each. Add grated lemon rind. Add flour mixture alternately with lemon juice, beginning and ending with flour. Fold in raisins and pecans with a spatula. Batter will be stiff.

In a separate bowl, add cream of tartar to egg whites and beat until stiff. Pour half of egg whites into batter. Using a large rubber spatula, fold in gently. Then fold in the other half.

Pour batter into the prepared pan and bake for approximately 2 hours, or until cake tests done and is lightly browned. Remove to cooling rack and let cool thoroughly before removing from pan. Invert onto a serving plate. Sprinkle with powdered sugar if desired. Keeps well.

MAKES 16 SERVINGS

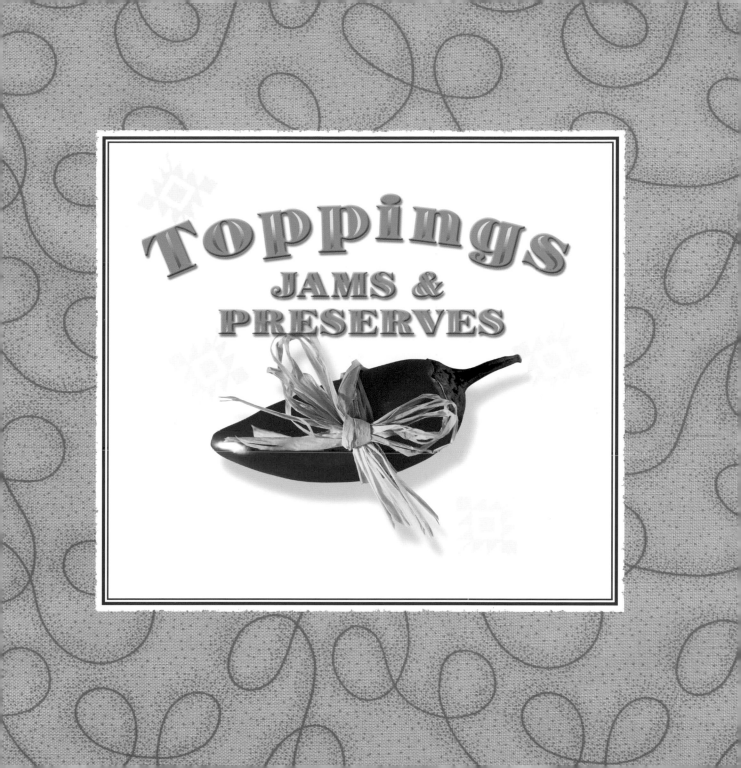

Toppings
JAMS & PRESERVES

Chameleon Chocolate Sauce

This versatile chocolate sauce is fabulous as is, or you can change its personality by stirring in a table-spoon of your favorite liqueur, such as Chambord for a raspberry flavor, or Grand Marnier for a sophisticated hint of orange. You can use this sauce a million different ways, hot or cold. We once used it as a layer in a trifle. Give a jar to your favorite ice-cream lover for his or her birthday; it's unbelievable over peppermint ice cream pie.

2 tablespoons butter

2 (1-ounce) squares unsweetened chocolate

1 cup powdered sugar

¾ cup (5-ounce can) evaporated milk

GIRLFRIEND GIFT

In a medium saucepan, melt butter and chocolate squares over low heat. Stir in powdered sugar and evap-orated milk. Raise heat and bring to a boil, stirring to keep from sticking. Remove from heat. Sauce will thicken as it cools.

MAKES ABOUT 1½ CUPS

Attach the following information with the gift or copy the tag on page 87:

TO USE CHAMELEON CHOCOLATE SAUCE:

Keep in a jar in the refrigerator. To use hot, reheat gently in the microwave on 70 percent power, stirring at 30-second intervals.

Pomegranate Jelly

Pomegranate trees are prolific and pretty in the neighborhoods of the Southwest. We like to dry the smaller fruit to decorate the mantel for holidays, and the seeds make a beautiful, purple jelly. Pair the fruits of your labor with a jar of Prickly Pear Jelly (page 62) for a jewel-toned gift of contrasting tastes and colors.

The only challenge with this recipe is removing the seeds from the fruit, and unfortunately, there is no secret trick. Just peel the thick skin away and pry the seeds out. We find it best to do this over the sink in case a seed is punctured and the ruby juice squirts out.

Pour the juice through. Do not squeeze the bag or the juice will become cloudy. Juice may be refrigerated at this point if making the jelly later.

Combine the juices and pectin in a deep saucepan and stir until dissolved. Bring to a rolling boil over high heat and stir in sugar. Bring to a rolling boil again and cook to 220 degrees on a candy thermometer or until thick jelly forms when the spoon is lifted from the pan, at least 15 minutes. Remove from heat and pour into hot, dry, sterilized jars. Seal the jars immediately with lids. Let cool. Will keep indefinitely under refrigeration.

MAKES 16 OUNCES
ABOUT 2 CUPS

IMPRESSIVE

Seeds of 1 large pomegranate	**1 ounce (2¾ tablespoons, or**
2 cups water	**½ box) powdered pectin**
⅛ cup lemon juice	**2½ cups sugar**

In a saucepan, cover the seeds with the water and bring to a boil. Cook for about 40 to 45 minutes, adding more water if needed, until you have about 1½ cups of deep purple juice.

Set a strainer lined with a jelly bag or a clean cotton tea towel (one that you don't mind staining) over a saucepan.

DECORATING TIP—*Simple and stylish, this jelly makes for the ultimate southwest gift. Cut brightly-patterned fabric into squares. Attach to the top of a jar with elastic cording. Finish by winding raffia around the elastic cording and tie it into a knot. Glue a colored marble into the center of the knot. A large flower makes an impressive alternative to fabric.*

Prickly Pear Jelly

This recipe came from Shirley Lohmann of Wilhoit, Arizona. She wisely suggests that you wear heavy gloves and use tongs if harvesting your own cactus fruit. In season, it's often possible to find the red prickly pear fruit, sans prickles, in the produce section of the supermarket.

3 large prickly pear fruits
1 ¹/₂ cups water
¹/₈ cup lemon juice
1 ounce (2³/₄ tablespoons, or ¹/₂ box) powdered pectin
2 ¹/₂ cups sugar

Festive

Combine fruit, rinsed well and halved, with water in a saucepan. Water should cover the fruit. Bring to a rolling boil for 20 minutes, or until the juice takes on a nice orange/pink tint. Add more water if needed during cooking.

Set a strainer lined with a jelly bag or a clean cotton tea towel (one that you don't mind staining) over a saucepan. Pour the juice through. Do not squeeze the bag, or the juice will become cloudy. Juice may be refrigerated at this point if making jelly later.

Combine the juices and pectin in a deep saucepan and stir until dissolved. Bring to a rolling boil over high heat, and stir in sugar. Bring to a rolling boil again and cook to 220 degrees on a candy thermometer, or until thick jelly forms when the spoon is lifted from the pan, at least 3 minutes. Remove from heat and pour into hot, dry, sterilized jars. Seal the jars immediately with lids. Let cool. Will keep indefinitely if refrigerated.

MAKES 16 OUNCES, ABOUT 2 CUPS

Bobbie's Strawberry Preserves

With this recipe for flawless preserves, you can have plump, perfectly suspended strawberries year-round. The syrup is great on anything from an Eggo to an English muffin or buttered biscuits. Like our Lemon Marmalade (page 65), it's a two-ingredient recipe that relies on technique. Don't even try to make this without a heavy-bottomed pan, and you must faithfully skim off all the foam when the preserves have finished cooking. Also, you must resist the urge to stir, because you want the berries to remain intact. Stirring makes them into mush.

3 cups whole strawberries, washed and hulled

3 cups sugar

In the bottom of a large, heavy-bottomed pot, pile the 3 cups of berries. On top of this, pile the 3 cups of sugar. Do not stir. Turn heat to medium and watch closely. As soon as little pink bubbles start to form at the edge of the sugar pile, set a timer for 20 minutes. Do not stir. The bubbles will foam up and fill the pot. At no time do you stir. In 20 minutes, the whole pot should be full of rolling pink bubbles. Turn off the heat. After the bubbles die down, skim all foam from the top of the mixture, but do not stir!

Pour hot preserves into a glass bowl. Cover with a plate and let sit at room temperature overnight. The strawberries will be fat and full of juice the next morning. Transfer to hot, dry, sterilized jars. Seal the jars immediately with lids. Let cool.

MAKES 3 ½-PINT JARS

DECORATING TIP—*Small jars, either clear glass or colored, will work just right. Purchase a basket, preferably with a handle, and using a colorful southwestern style bandana and your glue gun, gather the bandana around the bottom section of the basket. Glue as you go around the top section of the base of the basket. Wrap a coordinating ribbon around the handle of the basket to finish it. Place raffia in the basket and add southwestern touches of artificial cactus. Set the jars into the basket and you have a unique southwestern inspired hostess gift that can be used for muffins and scones later on.*

Easy Southwestern Lemon Curd

When lemons are abundant in the southwestern spring, it's time to make Lemonade, Lemon Curd, and Lemon Marmalade.

This recipe is the essence of lemon desserts. You will not believe the bright-yellow hue. Lemon curd is so versatile, but we like to fill little pastry shells with it and top them with whipped topping or whipped cream and toasted, sugared almonds. This has never failed to wow guests.

The trick to this recipe is using 70 percent power in the microwave. Eggs don't like high heat at any time.

6 beaten egg yolks

1 cup sugar

½ cup freshly squeezed lemon juice

1 stick butter, cut into small pieces

2 tablespoons packed lemon zest (the grated rind of 2 large or 4 small lemons)

In a 4-cup glass measure, whisk egg yolks, sugar, and lemon juice together well. Microwave at 70 percent power for 1 minute; reach into the microwave and whisk well. Microwave for 1 minute more and whisk again.

Microwave again for 2 minutes, whisk again, and see if the mixture will coat the back of a wooden spoon. If not, continue to microwave at 1-minute intervals at 70 percent power until the mixture passes this test.

Remove from microwave. Stir in butter, 1 piece at a time, until all is melted. Add zest and stir well. Let cool. Divide into 2 ½-pint jars for gift giving. Refrigerate.

Lime Curd Variation: Substitute freshly squeezed lime juice for the lemon juice, and lime zest for the lemon zest. Makes 2 1-cup containers.

Attach the following information with the gift or copy the tag on page 89:

TO USE EASY SOUTHWESTERN LEMON CURD

Enjoy on toast, scones, biscuits, or as a filling in baked tart shells (press thawed, pre-made pie dough into pastry shells, trim edges, and bake until lightly browned according to package directions. Sprinkle almonds lightly with sugar and toast in a toaster oven until fragrant. Watch closely. One hour before guests arrive, fill pastry shells with lemon curd; decorate with whipped topping, and refrigerate. Right before serving, sprinkle on the almonds).

Also great as a filling between cake layers, or mixed with whipped cream for a mousse-like dessert.

Lemon Curd will keep about 1 month in the refrigerator.

Lemon Marmalade

This is one of those recipes that is short on ingredients and long on technique. You will need a candy thermometer to clip to the side of the pan to measure the heat of the marmalade as it cooks. The results are worth the time, though, because this dark-golden marmalade is excellent.

3 pounds lemons
8 to 10 cups sugar

Slice lemons as thinly as possible, saving seeds. Discard ends. Tie all the seeds into a square of doubled cheesecloth, and put them in a large bowl with the lemons and water to cover. Let stand overnight.

Discard cheesecloth bag. Measure sliced lemons and seed water into a wide, deep skillet or Dutch oven. Add an equal amount of sugar. (For 8 cups of lemons and seed water, use 8 cups of sugar.) Cook over low heat until sugar dissolves. Raise heat to medium-high and cook, stirring and skimming foam, until temperature reaches 220 degrees. This may take about half an hour or longer.

Test for consistency by placing a little marmalade on a saucer and putting it in the freezer for about 5 minutes. The marmalade should just barely run when you tip the saucer. If it's too thin, continue cooking, testing often, until it passes this test.

Transfer mixture to hot, sterilized pint or ½-pint jars. Store in the refrigerator up to 1 month.

MAKES ABOUT 6 PINTS

DECORATING TIP—*Find a jar that will show off the marmalade's ingredients, like the chunky cubed one shown here. Use a rubber stamp to embellish the top of the lid, then add your own accents to it with paint pens. Cover your design with a water-based varnish to prevent scratches and tie a bow with raffia.*

Kumquat Marmalade

Cute little kumquats are not as common as some of the other citrus that are ubiquitous in the yards of many southwestern homes, but they are worth seeking out for this recipe. This marmalade is wonderful on a scone Easter morning. We also like to use whole kumquats and golden raisins in couscous for Easter dinner.

Eating raw whole kumquats is fine, but be sure to seed them for the marmalade, as seeds will affect the texture.

1 pound kumquats, halved and seeded

2 cups orange juice, preferably freshly squeezed

4 cups sugar

⅛ teaspoon grenadine

⅛ teaspoon angostura bitters

HOSTESS GIFT

In a blender or food processor, coarsely chop the halved kumquats. Transfer to a heavy-bottomed pan and add juice. Bring to a boil, stirring. Boil 20 minutes. Slowly stir in sugar until incorporated. Add grenadine and bitters. Continue to cook until the mixture has reached jelly stage, 220 degrees on a candy thermometer, or it coats the back of a spoon without dripping, about 15 minutes. Transfer to sterilized jars and seal. Refrigerate.

MAKES 4 ½-PINTS, 4 CUPS

DECORATING TIP—*A small terra-cotta saucer makes for a good earthy base to accompany the goods. Decorate the top of the jar lid with fabric and raffia. Apply a sticker to the center of the gift card, then attach it with elastic cording or raffia. Using E6000 glue, place the jar in the center of the saucer. Let dry until set. Embellish with greenery.*

Snacks &
FUN STUFF

Tempting Trail Mix

This tasty and colorful trail mix has become a staple in our pantries as well as on our hiking trips. It's a fast, easy gift for your active pals!

1 ½ **cups roasted unsalted almonds**

2 **cups roasted, salted pepitas (hulled, Mexican pumpkin seeds)**

2 **cups dried cranberries**

1 **cup dark chocolate chips (optional)**

Mix ingredients together. Store in an airtight container.

MAKES ABOUT 4 ½ TO 6 CUPS

Super Easy

EVERYBODY LOVES IT

DECORATING TIP— *Here's a gift basket that can be taken on the trail. Separate batches of mix into several cello bags, using twist ties and raffia for closure. With cowboy-themed fabric, sew 2 small pouches to hold the bags of the mix (use jute as a drawstring). Take a rectangular basket and line it with a traditional bandana. Fill with excelsior, then arrange bags into a balanced design with the two fabric bags on either end and the clear bags in the center. Tie a western hanging ornament to the center of the handle as a finishing touch.*

White Christmas Snack Mix

Sharon Cooper, our friend from Prescott, adapted this from a recipe she found in *Better Homes and Gardens®* magazine. What makes this snack so perfect for the winter holidays is the "snowy" effect from the white chocolate with the colored fruit peeking through. It may be the only snow we get in the deserts of the Southwest.

2 cups honey-nut flavored O-shaped cereal,
    such as Cheerios
¾ cup raisins, golden raisins, Craisins,
    or dried cranberries
¾ cup dried cherries
½ cup dried apricots, cut into quarters
1 cup broken pecans
½ cup shelled, dry-roasted pistachios
2½ cups bite-size frosted shredded wheat cereal
2 cups broken graham crackers, or cinnamon
    or chocolate graham crackers, or a combination
    of both
1 pound white chocolate chips or vanilla baking bar
½ cup whipping cream
2 tablespoons light-colored corn syrup
1 tablespoon vanilla extract
1 cup miniature marshmallows (optional)

Prepare a 9 x 13-inch baking pan or roasting pan by lining with waxed paper.

In a large bowl, stir together cereal, raisins, cherries, apricots, pecans, pistachios, shredded wheat, and graham crackers. In a medium-size saucepan, combine white chocolate chips or baking bar, cream, corn syrup, and vanilla. Stir continuously over low heat until melted and combined. The mixture will be very thick.

Remove from heat and let cool a few minutes, then quickly fold into the dry ingredients, stirring to combine. Add the marshmallows, if using, and stir again. Spread into baking pan and cover with waxed paper. Let stand overnight or up to 12 hours. Break into pieces.

MAKES ABOUT 14 TO 15 CUPS

Festive

Colorful Citrus Circles

Many backyard gardeners tend citrus trees in the Southwest. These trees can be so prolific that using all the fruit becomes a challenge. Call in the food dehydrator! Dried citrus slices combined with other dried foods such as cinnamon sticks and bay leaves are popular at craft shows. We bring these natural objects to the wall of your kitchen in a different way.

Citrus slices
Chiles or peppers
Bay leaves
Cinnamon sticks
Star anise
Nuts in the shell
Raffia
Cornhusks
Hot glue

Dont Eat This! Slice large grapefruit, oranges, or lemons into ¼-inch rounds. Dry in food dehydrator, following the manufacturer's directions. Drying can take a couple of days for slices this thick. Set dried slices aside.

Dehydrate a variety of sizes and colors of chiles and peppers. Try poblanos (these are the largest and will take the longest), habaneros, Hungarian peppers, serrano chiles, green chiles, jalapeños, anchos—whatever you can find in the produce section. Use at least 3 chiles per wreath.

Once the fruit and chiles are dry, assemble along with cinnamon sticks, bay leaves, star anise, nuts in the shell, or whatever else you can find around your kitchen or in a craft store. Bits of raffia and cornhusk can also be used. Plug in the glue gun and set your imagination free.

Start by arranging the fruit slices so they overlap and form a circle about 10 inches in diameter, creating the wreath base. Alternate with one slice on the bottom, the next slice on top, etc., placing a spot of hot glue on the edges to hold them together. These dry items are very light, so it only takes a small bit of glue to hold things firmly in place. If you have enough slices, you can make several layers of citrus rounds, using the largest ones at the bottom and smaller ones on top.

Next, use the chiles, sticks, leaves, nuts, and other objects to make a pleasing arrangement for decorating the top of the wreath. Make sure you like the placement and plan out the entire wreath decor before you glue any of the decorations down. Pay attention to the various colors you are adding, and make sure the colors are balanced in an appealing way. Remember—less is more. Don't get too much stuff on the wreath!

The dried citrus will have lots of holes that can be used for hanging the wreath, or you can make a hanger by knotting a length of raffia through a slice and tying a loop in the top. You can always add a bow to the wreath as well. Use leftover supplies for Harvest Lapel Pins.

Harvest Lapel Pins

Make simple, charming lapel pins by adding 1-inch pin backs to small pieces of dried fruit leftover from making Colorful Citrus Circles. Your friends will be wearing aromatherapy! With a glue gun and the small, dried end pieces of lemons, oranges, or grapefruit as the base of your pin, glue on 2-inch cinnamon sticks, bay leaves, and star anise, decorating with tiny bits of raffia, or trace 3 bay leaves onto thin cardboard or chipboard and cut a backing to glue to the backs of the leaves. Fan the leaves and connect with a spot of glue. Top the leaf base with a ½-inch piece of cinnamon stick or one star anise. Glue the pin back on last.

We like to wrap these in a bit of tissue and then in plain brown paper cut from a grocery bag. Make an envelope shape, fold down the flap, and hot-glue it down with a small dried orange slice on top.

Dont Eat This!

Many-Bean Topiary Tree

We often enjoy 13- or 15-bean soup from the packages you buy already mixed. The dried beans are so beautiful: the yellow and green peas, red kidneys, white great Northerns, black-eyed wonders, ocher garbanzos or chick peas, ebony black beans. Unfortunately, they lose their grandeur when cooked, so Kim wanted to find a way to enjoy their beauty without cooking them. She was so surprised to find only 14 varieties of beans in a bag that said it held 15! We still laugh about that, years later, when we marvel at the topiary tree that stands in the living room. It also becomes part of the tabletop Christmas tree collection during the holidays.

Dont Eat This!

1 or 2 bags of 13 or 15-bean soup mix,
    sorted by type
1 florist foam-base topiary tree in the shape
    of your choice, at least 15 inches tall
Pine cones (if your topiary tree has a base that
    needs to be covered)
1 tiny pine cone, a small dried pomegranate,
    a large nut, or one other item for the
    finial topper
Hot glue

Use muffin tins or ice cube trays to sort the beans. If the topiary has a base that is meant to look like a pot or basket, cut the "petals" from the pine cone and glue them onto the base in rows. Cover the top of the basket with a single layer of small white beans, glued down individually.

Now, working your way up from the bottom of the cone that forms the tree, glue on rows of beans all around the diameter of the tree, using the larger beans at the bottom. Alternate colors and shapes with each row. For example, start with a row of Great Northern beans, then two rows of kidneys, a single row of black beans, a row of garbanzos, a double row of pintos, a row of white limas, a double row of orange split peas, and so forth. The textures and colors should vary for interest and eye appeal as you progress up the tree. Glue a tiny pinecone or other small natural object on the very top as the finial.

Tijuana Tidbits

Imagine Kim's delight when she got a gift from the kitchen of our friend Sharon Cooper for her birthday! It was a southwestern version of homemade Cracker Jacks. Sharon adapted the recipe from the *Ladies' Home Journal Holiday Issue* of January 1998. We love it!

4 cups broken, bite-size pieces of restaurant-quality
  corn tortilla chips

3 cups Crispix, Chex, or other similar square-shaped
  cereal

8 to 9 cups popped popcorn

1 (12-ounce) can salted mixed nuts

½ cup white corn syrup

½ cup butter

½ cup brown sugar, packed

1 tablespoon powdered pure red chile

½ teaspoon cinnamon

⅛ to ¼ teaspoon cayenne (optional, use for
  a bit of bite)

Preheat oven to 250 degrees and coat a jelly roll pan with nonstick spray.

In a very large bowl, combine the chips, cereal, popcorn, and nuts, and spread the mix on the coated jelly roll pan. In a medium saucepan, combine corn syrup, butter, sugar, and spices. Heat to a rolling boil. Pour over the cereal mixture and stir to coat well. Transfer to a large roasting pan. Place in oven for 1 hour, stirring every 15 to 20 minutes. Cool on 2 cookie sheets lined with waxed paper.

MAKES ABOUT 18 CUPS

EVERYBODY
LOVES IT

Butterbeer Mix for Muggle Kids

If your kids are Harry Potter fans—and whose aren't?—they will love this mix stirred into a mug of hot apple juice or cider. Mack Walker, age 11, recognized this immediately as Butterbeer, which Harry, Hermione, and Ron always warm up with in their hangout, The Three Broomsticks in Hogsmeade.

Today's big mugs usually hold about 1½ cups of water, so increase the amount of mix used accordingly.

3 cups packed light brown sugar

½ cup butter (1 stick, softened—no substitute)

2 tablespoons honey, preferably desert flower honey

1 tablespoon Mexican vanilla

1 tablespoon rum extract

1 teaspoon ground cinnamon

½ teaspoon ground allspice

½ teaspoon ground nutmeg

In the bowl of an electric mixer, combine brown sugar, butter, honey, extracts, and spices. Beat at medium speed until smooth and consistent. Pack into a jar or plastic container with a tight lid.

To give as gifts, spoon 1 cup mix each into 2 1-cup containers. Attach the following instruction or copy the tag on page 89:

TO USE BUTTERBEER MIX FOR MUGGLE KIDS:
Store in refrigerator and use within 3 months. Using 1 to 2 teaspoons mix per cup of beverage, stir into hot apple cider or juice to make Butterbeer for Harry Potter fans. Or use in any hot beverage: hot milk, coffee, tea, cafe au lait. To make Hot Buttered Rum, stir 1 teaspoonful into 1 cup hot water and 1 ounce rum.

Great-4-Kids

Aztec Hot Chocolate Mix

You can put together this gift mix in five minutes flat. It's spiced chocolate with flavors reminiscent of the famous Mexican varieties. The Aztecs liked a little canela (cinnamon) in their beverages. The entire finished recipe, which makes about 2½ cups or 10 servings, fits in a sandwich-size zip-top bag. We like to pop the mixture into a smartly decorated brown paper bag. However, you can also divvy this up into individual servings—use ¼ cup mix for each to package with a mug.

2⅓ **cups powdered milk**
½ **cup sugar**
1 **tablespoon flour**
¼ **cup cocoa**
¼ **teaspoon salt**
1 **teaspoon ground cinnamon**
⅛ **teaspoon ground allspice**

Combine all ingredients in a large bowl and mix well, until mixture is a uniform color.

Attach the following instructions with the gift or copy the tag on page 85:

TO MAKE AZTEC HOT CHOCOLATE:

Put ¼ cup mix (about 3 tablespoons) in your favorite mug and fill with water. Stir well. Microwave on high 1 minute. Add 1 or 2 drops vanilla (optional) and stir well again.

Great-4-Kids   Super Easy

Cornhusk Wreath

Kim made this wreath several years ago and it has been hanging in her kitchen ever since. Although it has the obvious Christmas applications, it would also be nice on a front door in the fall, or just remove the chiles and replace them with dried spring or summer flowers—this piece has no seasonal limitations.

1 (12- or 15-inch) straw craft wreath, with the
   plastic shrink-wrap intact
1 package dried corn husks
Straight pins
A bit of string
2 or 3 fresh green chiles or dried red chiles with
   stems

Dont Eat This!

Flatten out a corn husk and bring the ends together (but do not crease) so the husk forms a flattened loop. Place straight pins through both layers in each corner of the matched edges and pin the looped husk to the wreath base, right through the plastic, so that the edges go across the width of the wreath, along the circle. Cover the width of the wreath base by using two rows of looped husks, if necessary. Working in the same direction, overlap the next row of husks so the looped end covers the pinned edge of the previous husk. Repeat until the entire wreath is covered with husk loops in a pattern that is pleasing to the eye, making sure that all the pinned edges are hidden.

Tie string around the stems of the chiles so that they collect in a bunch. Attach the chiles to the wreath with straight pins so chiles hang down in the center of the wreath.

Fourth-of-July Lemonade, Two Ways

A cool beverage can be your summer signature dish for potlucks! Judy's mom, Bobbie Trower, has a giant lemon tree in her Arizona backyard and has become a connoisseur of lemonade recipes. Here are her two favorite ways to make it, both of which are unusual.

Mashed Lemonade

4 lemons
3/4 cup sugar
4 cups water

Slice lemons very thinly into a glass container, removing seeds. Pour sugar over lemon slices and let sit for 10 minutes to macerate. Add water. Use a potato masher or the back of a spoon to mash up lemons. Drain liquid into a pitcher and serve over ice.

MAKES 4 SERVINGS

Blender Lemonade

2 lemons
1 cup sugar
6 cups water, divided use

Slice lemons thinly, discarding ends. Put in blender container with sugar and 2 cups of water. Blend until slushy. Strain into a large pitcher. (Strain promptly or the water leaches out too much bitter oil from the peel.) Pour 4 more cups water over pulp in the strainer. Discard pulp. Stir lemonade and serve over ice.

MAKES 6 SERVINGS

Embellished Nuts

Nuts can be sweet or savory. Either type is wonderful in a salad, or package nuts in a special serving bowl for a charming hostess gift. The sweet version is nice at a cocktail party or on a dessert tray. One of our favorite chef pals, Norman Fierros, uses the sweet-hot version (which inspired our recipe) in a luscious Primavera Salad.

1 cup pecan or walnut halves
2 tablespoons butter, softened

SWEET:
1 teaspoon cinnamon mixed with 1 teaspoon
   granulated sugar
1 teaspoon brown sugar
1 teaspoon granulated sugar

SAVORY:
2 teaspoons Grilled Vegetable Seasoning Mix
   (recipe page 20)

In a heavy-bottomed skillet, heat nuts over medium high for about 2 minutes, until they are warmed through and are just about to become fragrant. Add butter and stir, coating the nuts.

For sweet nuts: Sprinkle with cinnamon-sugar mixture and brown sugar. Stir to coat all the nuts, and continue to cook over medium-high heat for about 2 minutes or until the cinnamon releases its fragrance. Turn out onto a shallow baking sheet and allow the nuts to partially cool, about 4 to 5 minutes. Sprinkle with 1 teaspoon granulated sugar and roll the nuts to evenly coat.

For savory nuts: Sprinkle with Grilled Vegetable Seasoning Mix. Stir to coat all the nuts, and continue to cook over medium-high heat for about 2 minutes or until the seasonings releases their fragrance. Immediately remove to a bowl.

Allow the nuts to cool before serving or packaging.

EACH VERSION MAKES 1 CUP

Soothing Citrus Bath Tea

We call ourselves the "Spa Maidens" during our annual trek with girlfriends to Palm Springs to bask in the mineral waters. Any girlfriend would love to receive this gift, which was inspired by a present from our sister Spa Maiden, Sally Stearman. The citrus and the rosemary are from our yards.

Look for the fusible fill-your-own tea bags at herb and health food stores.

¼ cup dried grapefruit peel and ¼ cup dried
   orange peel (or any combination of citrus
   to equal ½ cup)
¼ cup dried rosemary
¼ cup oatmeal

Combine the peels, herbs, and oatmeal in a muslin bag or very large fusible fill-your-own tea bag.

Attach a gift tag with the following instructions or copy the tag on page 89:

TO USE SOOTHING CITRUS BATH TEA:
Tie this bag to the tub faucet or toss the tea bag in the water and draw a bath, so that the water runs over the bag. The bath tea will soften the water, impart a fresh, clean aroma, and banish fatigue.

MAKES ENOUGH FOR 1 BATH

JUDY WALKER is the author of *Savory Southwest: Prize-Winning Recipes from The Arizona Republic* and *Simple Southwestern Cooking: Quick Recipes for Today's Busy Lifestyle*, both from Northland Publishing, as well as countless newspaper articles on food and cooking. She is a member of the Arizona Culinary Hall of Fame and a founding member of the Phoenix chapter of Les Dames Escoffier. She was food editor for *The Arizona Republic* for many years before moving to New Orleans with her husband, Dave, and son, Mack. She is now the homes and gardens writer for the *New Orleans Times-Picayune*.

KIM MACEACHERN is an attorney living in Phoenix. She loves conducting mediations and serving as a Judge Pro Tem for Maricopa County and the City of Phoenix. Kim is Vice President of the Governing Board of the Arizona Center for the Blind and Visually Impaired. She also occasionally teaches college level courses, but her main interest is in keeping up with the busy schedule of her daughter Melanie and her incredibly brainy husband Doug MacEachern. She and Judy Walker are the co-authors of *Chips, Dips, and Salsas* and *Southwestern Soup, Stews, and Skillet Suppers*, also from Northland Publishing.

TO MAKE LENTIL RICE SOUP

In a large soup pot, heat 1 tablespoon olive oil and sauté 1 chopped carrot for 3 minutes, stirring constantly. Add herb mix and cook for about 1 minute more. Add 8 cups water and soup mix. Stir to combine. Simmer 45 minutes. Add vinegar, salt, and pepper to taste.

MAKES 8 SERVINGS

TO MAKE HEARTY BARLEY SOUP

Heat 6 cups chicken broth (or 6 cups water and 2 chicken or beef bouillon cubes) to boiling. Add soup mix and simmer 30 minutes. Add 2 chopped carrots, 2 chopped celery stalks, $1\frac{1}{2}$ cups shredded cabbage, and 1 ($14\frac{1}{2}$-ounce) can tomatoes with juice. Simmer 20 minutes.

MAKES 6 SERVINGS

TO MAKE POTATO AND GREEN CHILE SOUP

Dice 2 slices of bacon (or crumble $\frac{1}{2}$ a pound of bulk sausage) into a medium saucepan. Cook until almost browned. Chop the onion and add it along with the undrained green chiles. Cook until onion is translucent. (Drain grease if necessary.) Peel and dice potatoes; add with broth and salt and pepper to taste. Cover and cook over medium heat 10 to 15 minutes, until potato is tender. Lower heat to simmer and add milk. Mash a few potatoes against the side of the pot if you want a thicker soup. Cook until hot; serve.

MAKES 4 SERVINGS

TO MAKE RAINBOW SOUP

Chop 3 large or 5 small carrots. In a stockpot over medium heat, sauté the carrots in 1 tablespoon olive oil. Add the contents of the jar and the seasoning mix. Add 7 cups of water and simmer 20 minutes for lentils, 1 hour for split peas.

MAKES 6 SERVINGS

TO MAKE BLACK BEAN CHILI

Chop the onion and combine it with all ingredients in a large, deep pot. Cover and simmer for 30 minutes to 1 hour, adding more liquid if needed, or place ingredients in a slow cooker on low heat for up to 8 hours. Serve with salsa, chopped onion, and shredded cheese if desired.

MAKES 8 TO 10 SERVINGS

TO MAKE WHITE CHILI

In a large, deep pot, heat 1 tablespoon olive oil and sauté 1 chopped onion, 2 cloves minced garlic, contents of seasoning packet, and 4 boneless, skinless chicken breasts, diced. Add a 4-ounce can green chiles, 3 cans chicken broth, and 2 cans drained white beans. Bring to a boil, reduce heat, and simmer 20 minutes. Serve topped with shredded Monterey Jack cheese. Can also be garnished with chopped cilantro, sour cream, and salsa.

MAKES 8 SERVINGS

TO MAKE SUPERIOR CHILI

Heat 2 tablespoons oil in a Dutch oven.
Chop 1 large onion and sauté with 2 minced garlic
cloves. Add 1 pound ground beef and cook until
browned. Drain all fat. Sprinkle in chili seasoning mix
and stir well. Add 2 (14$\frac{1}{2}$-ounce) cans tomatoes and 1
cup water or broth. Cook at least 30 minutes.

MAKES 5 TO 6 SERVINGS

TO MAKE PICKLED GARLIC SALAD DRESSING

For the best salad dressing in the world,
combine several cloves of this garlic, finely chopped, and
a little bit of the liquid from the jar with white wine and
balsamic vinegar, extra-virgin olive oil (1 part vinegar
to 3 parts oil), and a dab of Dijon mustard. Serve it
over a salad of greens, goat cheese, toasted nuts,
and chopped pear or apple.

TO MAKE SEASONED GRILLED VEGETABLES

Slice veggies about $\frac{1}{8}$-inch thick and lightly spray both sides
with oil. Sprinkle with seasoning mix on both sides. Starting with
denser vegetables first, adding those with higher moisture
content later, grill over medium heat about 10 to 15 minutes,
turning once or twice as needed. Mushrooms, except portabellas,
take about half as long as other vegetables to grill.

SEASONS SEVERAL POUNDS OF VEGETABLES

TO USE
SOUTHWEST SEASONING MIX

Sprinkle mix on generously
to enliven chicken dishes, salsas, croutons,
soups, and salads.

TO USE COPPER QUEEN RUB

Before grilling,
rub meat all over with this powder.
Let sit for 5 to 10 minutes and
then grill as usual.

SEASONS SEVERAL POUNDS OF MEAT

TO MAKE ENCHILADA SAUCE

Combine $\frac{1}{4}$ cup olive oil and $\frac{1}{2}$ cup flour in a 2-quart
saucepan over medium-high heat. Stir to form a paste or
roux. Cook until mixture just begins to brown. Add seasoning
mix and stir to combine. Slowly whisk in 4 cups water,
incorporating each addition to make a smooth, gravylike
consistency. Stir in $\frac{1}{4}$ cup cider vinegar. Bring to a gentle
simmer, stirring continuously, and cook for 10 minutes.

MAKES 5 CUPS

TO MAKE SLOPPY JOSÉS

In a large skillet, brown 1 pound ground beef over medium-high heat with a 4-ounce can of diced green chiles. When meat is browned, drain carefully. To the meat mixture add 1 tablespoon Sloppy José Mix, a 6-ounce can of tomato paste, and 1½ cups water. Mix well. Cook 10 minutes over low heat. Serve on hamburger buns.   MAKES 4 TO 6 SERVINGS

TO MAKE ORANGE COUSCOUS

Heat 1 cup water
to boiling in a small saucepan. Stir in contents
of this bag and 2 tablespoons butter. Cook for 2 minutes.
Cover, remove from heat, and let stand 5 minutes.
Fluff with a fork and enjoy!

MAKES 4 TO 6 SERVINGS

TO MAKE REAL CORNBREAD

Preheat oven to 400 degrees.
Combine 1¼ cups milk and ¼ cup vegetable oil in a large bowl.
Add 2 eggs and beat well. Dump cornbread mix into a separate
large bowl. Stir egg mixture into cornbread mix until smooth.
Pour into a greased 9 x 13 pan, a 10-inch cast-iron skillet,
or 10 to 12 individual cast-iron molds. Bake 30 minutes for pans,
20 minutes for molds, until medium golden brown.

MAKES 10 TO 12 SERVINGS

TO MAKE CHILI BEER BREAD

Preheat oven to 400 degrees. Pour bread mix into
a bowl and make a well in the center. Pour in 12 ounces of
beer at room temperature. Stir lightly, just until blended.
Scrape into a well-greased loaf pan and bake 20 minutes.
Remove from oven and pour ¼ cup melted butter over the
top. Bake 20 minutes longer.

MAKES 1 LOAF

TO MAKE PUFF PANCAKES

Preheat oven to 450 degrees. Put 2 tablespoons butter
in each of 2 (9-inch) pie plates, and place in oven to melt.
Combine pancake mix, 4 eggs, and ⅔ cup milk in a blender
and mix. Batter will be thin. Pour into pie plates and bake 18
minutes, or until pancakes puff up and brown. Remove from
oven and sprinkle with lemon juice and powdered sugar,
or top with fresh fruit mixed with a little sour cream.
Cut into wedges and serve immediately.

MAKES 2 LARGE PANCAKES OR 4 SERVINGS

TO MAKE AZTEC HOT CHOCOLATE

Put ¼ cup mix (about 3 tablespoons)
in your favorite mug and fill with water. Stir well.
Microwave on high 1 minute.
Add 1 or 2 drops vanilla (optional)
and stir well again.

TO MAKE OATMEAL BARS IN A JAR

Preheat oven to 350 degrees. Pour contents of jar into a medium-size mixing bowl. Add $\frac{1}{3}$ cup oil, 1 large egg, and 1 teaspoon vanilla. Stir to combine. Press into a greased 8 x 8-inch baking pan. Bake for 20 to 30 minutes or until brown and set in the middle.

MAKES 16 SMALL OR 9 LARGE BARS

TO MAKE SAND ART BARS

Preheat oven to 350 degrees. Dump contents of jar into a large bowl. Add 3 eggs, $\frac{1}{2}$ cup oil, and 1 teaspoon vanilla. Mix well. Spread into a greased 9 x 13-inch pan. Bake for 27 to 32 minutes.

MAKES 15 TO 18 BARS

TO MAKE OLD-FASHIONED OAT CAKES

Preheat oven to 375 degrees. Empty bag of mix into a medium-sized bowl. With a pastry cutter or 2 knives, cut in $\frac{3}{4}$ cup butter (1 $\frac{1}{2}$ sticks) until the mixture has a crumbly texture. Add $\frac{1}{2}$ cup water or milk and stir with a fork until dough just clings together. Divide dough into thirds and roll out each portion on a lightly floured board to $\frac{1}{8}$-inch thick. Cut into 2-inch squares and place 1 inch apart on an ungreased cookie sheet. Bake 10 to 15 minutes, until lightly browned.

MAKES 4 TO 5 DOZEN OAT CAKES

TO MAKE PECAN BUTTERSCOTCH BARS

Preheat oven to 350 degrees. Pour contents of jar into a medium-size mixing bowl. Add $\frac{1}{3}$ cup oil, 1 large egg, and 1 teaspoon vanilla. Stir to combine. Press into a greased 8 x 8-inch baking dish. Bake for 20 to 30 minutes or until brown and set in the middle.

MAKES 16 SMALL OR 9 LARGE BARS

TO USE
CHAMELEON CHOCOLATE SAUCE

Keep in a jar in the refrigerator. To use hot, reheat gently in the microwave on 70 percent power, stirring at 30-second intervals.

TO USE EASY SOUTHWESTERN LEMON CURD

Enjoy on toast, scones, biscuits, or as a filling in baked tart shells (press thawed, pre-made pie dough into pastry shells, trim edges, and bake until lightly browned according to package directions. Sprinkle almonds lightly with sugar and toast in a toaster oven until fragrant. Watch closely. One hour before guests arrive, fill pastry shells with lemon curd; decorate with whipped topping, and refrigerate. Right before serving, sprinkle on the almonds). Also great as a filling between cake layers, or mixed with whipped cream for a mousse-like dessert. Lemon Curd will keep about 1 month in the refrigerator.

TO MAKE BUTTERMILK CURRANT SCONES

Preheat oven to 450 degrees. Put dry mixture into a large bowl. Use a knife to cut 6 tablespoons of very cold butter into small pieces, adding it to the mix. Use a pastry cutter or 2 knives to cut the butter into the mixture until it resembles coarse crumbs. Beat together 2 eggs with milk and add to the mixture along with currants. Mix until the liquid is completely incorporated. Dough will be very soft.

Turn out onto a heavily floured surface and knead gently, turning the dough 5 or 6 times. Pat out with your hands into a 9-inch square. Cut into 3 rectangles. Cut each rectangle in half, then cut each half into triangles. Place on a lightly greased jelly roll pan 1 inch apart. Brush tops with 1 tablespoon of milk and sprinkle with 1 tablespoon of sugar. Bake 12 to 15 minutes, until tops are lightly golden. MAKES 12 SCONES

TO USE BUTTERBEER MIX FOR MUGGLE KIDS

Store in refrigerator and use within 3 months. Using 1 to 2 teaspoons mix per cup of beverage, stir into hot apple cider or juice to make Butterbeer for Harry Potter fans; or use in any hot beverage: hot milk, coffee, tea, cafe au lait. To make Hot Buttered Rum, stir 1 teaspoonful into 1 cup hot water and 1 ounce rum.

TO MAKE BEAN, PASTA, AND SAUSAGE SOUP

Heat soup to boiling. Add pasta and simmer 10 minutes. Serve topped with Parmesan.

MAKES 10 SERVINGS

TO USE SOOTHING CITRUS BATH TEA

Tie this bag to the tub faucet
or toss the tea bag in the water and draw a bath,
so that the water runs over the bag.
The bath tea will soften the water,
impart a fresh, clean aroma,
and banish fatigue.

MAKES ENOUGH FOR 1 BATH